The Electronic Office

Malcolm Peltu

CW01572590

THE ELECTRONIC OFFICE

Malcolm Peltu

Cartoons by Mollusc

ARIEL BOOKS
BRITISH BROADCASTING CORPORATION

Dedication

I dedicate this book to my father, Louis Peltu, who died on the day I finished it. Also to the nursing and medical staff at the New End, Coppetts Wood and Royal Free hospitals in London. Their caring for my father allowed me to work on the book in some peace of mind. They are a tribute to the British National Health Service.

Acknowledgements

To David Allen, producer of the BBC Computer Literacy project, for asking me to write this book.

To Charles Elton, Meyer Solomon and Mike Cocker of the BBC for their friendly encouragement.

To Harry Otway and my colleagues who worked on the project within the European Commission's INSIS office technology programme that culminated in the book *New Office Technology: Human and Organisational Aspects* (Frances Pinter, 1983; Ablex in the US). They helped to sharpen my awareness that the electronic office is more about people than technology.

To Pinky and Penny for their all-night vigils.

Malcolm Peltu
Chiswick
5 September 1983

Published by the British Broadcasting Corporation
35 Marylebone High Street, London W1M 4AA

Typeset by Phoenix Photosetting, Chatham, Kent
Printed in Great Britain by Mackays of Chatham Ltd, Kent

Set in 10/11 point Linotron Ehrhardt

ISBN 0 563 21056 7

Welcome to the electronic office

All office life is here

The Electronic Office will be of interest and use to anyone who has an office job; runs a business (big or small); works from home (or who might do so in the future). It will also be of value to those who rely on the results of office work to receive some service, such as a pension, unemployment benefit or an answer to an enquiry. The main theme of the book is the way computer-based information technology can assist and change office work.

Offices are seldom static. As people change, office activities change; as organisations evolve, office procedures evolve. Technology must support this dynamic nature of office work, not hinder it. The exciting new technological options bursting onto the market place could fizzle out unless they are implemented in ways which satisfy the real needs of those who the technology should serve. This book is not only a plain-language guide to what the technology can do, but also places the technology in its broader social and human context. After reading *The Electronic Office* you should have increased confidence in being able to handle the technology as it affects your own life.

To begin at the beginning

Like the classic film *Sunset Boulevard*, the book is built around a body and a pool.

The body of the book (Chapters 1 to 6) describes what new office technology does, how it will be used in offices, its effects on organisations and jobs – and how people can control its impact. The body should be looked at as a whole.

The pool should be dipped into – – as a refresher; to find out a bit more background and history; and to check the meaning of some words. You should still, however, begin at the beginning – with the Introduction. This provides an overview of the subjects dealt with in the rest of the book and introduces key concepts which are the foundations of the electronic office.

Contents

Introduction:
A new era of office work

Where have all the quill pens gone?

Most people with a job in industrialised countries do some form of office work. The routines and social activities of offices are part of the modern way of life. Office blocks are a feature of urban landscapes. The tools of the office trade, like typewriters and telephones have become as symbolic of work as were the plough and spinning wheel, steam engine and automated production line in previous ages. But it hasn't always been like this.

There was a time when the vast majority of people worked in agriculture, mining and other *primary* industries which were directly involved in reaping the benefits of natural resources; in less industrialised countries this is still true. The quill pen was then the symbol of the laborious, but relatively comfortable, office work carried out by small groups of scribes, clerks and mathematicians.

Then came a rash of inventions. From Jethro Tull's seed grower in 1701 to the twentieth century combine harvester and tractor, agricultural methods were transformed. By the 1980s, less than 3% of the workforce in some countries were concerned with primary industries, although they were meeting far greater demands than at the time when over 50% of people worked in agriculture.

The steam engine triggered the Industrial Revolution in the late eighteenth century. It provided power for manufacturing processes, and led to the development of the railways and improved means of product distribution. This created new ways of living (in cities rather than small villages in the countryside) and new ways of working (in manufacturing factories and mills rather than on the land). In some countries more than 50% of the population were engaged in manufacturing industries by the mid-nineteenth century. A third type of activity has now emerged as a major source of employment and wealth creation. In these, people and companies offer a *service*, rather than manufacturing a product, growing vegetables, digging coal, etc. Nurses and teachers, shop assistants and chefs, bankers and insurance salesmen, actors and journalists, architects and scientists, and armies of office workers have been the beneficiaries of the expansion in services jobs.

An oasis on the move

Figure 1 illustrates the employment patterns in the UK from 1841 to 1982. It shows the trends in the percentage of the population employed in primary, manufacturing and services industries. These trends are continuing strongly in all industrialised countries. Employment in primary industries now involves a smallish percentage of the population (the UK percentage is much smaller than for many other European countries). After peaking in the first part of the twentieth century, employment in manufacturing industry began to lose its dominance. And since the 1960s, service industries have become the major employers.

The nature of employment and people's jobs have therefore been subject to continuous change. At times like the Industrial Revolution, those changes sent shock-waves throughout society. In primary and manufacturing industries, technological innovation has maintained a dynamic pace for centuries. Office work, however, has remained an oasis of relative tranquillity.

The quill pen has been turned into a museum piece and inventions like the typewriter, telephone, telex and photocopying have made important changes to office routines. By the 1980s, however, over ten times more had been invested in equipment to support each factory worker than that spent on each office worker. Productivity in office work remained almost static for many decades while productivity in manufacturing industry regularly doubled within ten years.

Enter now cheap computing and chips with everything. The typewriter is threatened with the same fate as the quill pen. The office scene is moving quickly into the twenty-first century. A new era in office work beckons. This book is a window on that new world.

Goings-on in the office

Before looking at the future of offices, we must try to answer the questions: What is an office? What is office work?

Offices come in many shapes and sizes. Office work means different things to different people. Where is the common thread?

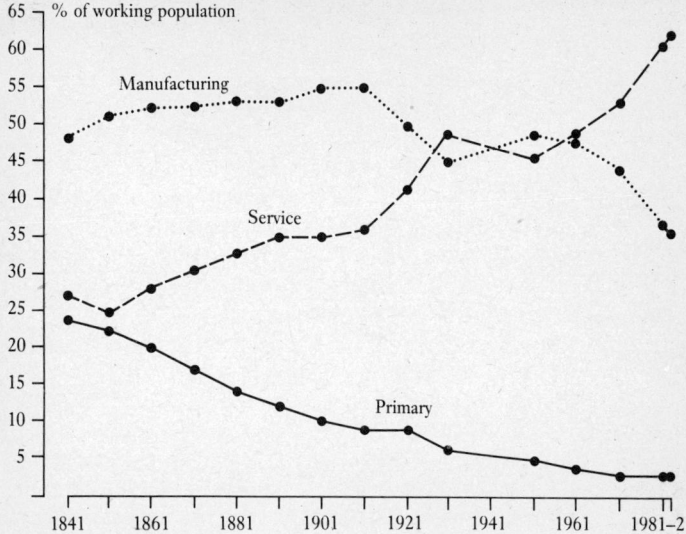

Figure 1: Employment trends in Great Britain, 1841 to 1982
(Source: *Manpower Implications of Micrelectronic Technology*, UK Department of Employment, HMSO, 1979 plus further Department of Employment statistics.)

●—●—● Services employment, including office work
●······●······● Manufacturing industry
●——●——● Primary industries (mainly agriculture and mining)

An 'office' could be the backroom of a small shop; the local branch of a large bank; a sleek air-conditioned, typing pool; a musty old accounts office; the plush suite of a chief executive; the cramped and cluttered laboratory of a research worker; the comfortable home of a computer programmer. You could go on endlessly adding to this list. A person who travels a lot may even use his or her briefcase, a dictating machine, a portable type-writer (or portable computer!) as a moving office.

To some people 'office work' means the nitty-gritty grind of recording information; to others, it means the nerve-tingling decision-making of big business power games. Office work consists of typing letters; filing documents; checking stock; paying welfare benefits; finding jobs for people; analysing information to make decisions; copying documents; answering the telephone; making appointments; attending meetings; printing salary cheques; organising, re-organising and re-re-organising departments and working procedures . . . once again, a list without end.

Offices are also about making friends, forming groups, chatting informally, working hard sometimes, relaxing at other times. In general, offices provide a relatively pleasant working environment compared to the rigidly structured and closely monitored nature of manufacturing jobs. Even in office jobs that seem dull, there are usually some opportunities for variations to the daily routine. Office workers also usually have some discretion in deciding how to do their job, unlike workers on a production line who have to follow precisely the same routines every day.

Despite this diversity, there is a common thread – *information*. Like the air we breathe, information is all around us but we are seldom aware of its existence as such. Information is the raw material of office work. Memos, reports, letters, telephone conversations, diagrams, tape and video recordings are all forms of information. Office workers do lots of things to that information – filing, sorting, listening, passing on, calculating, shredding, copying, updating, and so on.

Information work goes on in all sorts of offices. And new electronic technologies which handle all types of information will transform how, where and when office work can be carried out.

A many-splendoured thing

Information is a many-splendoured thing. The bright petals of a flower are an information signal to attract bees. The purr of a cat and the chirping of a cricket transmit information. Tom-tom drums and American Indian smoke signals are basic forms of human telecommunications. Everywhere, people devise and use ingenious ways of communicating information.

Many different technologies have been invented for handling particular types of information. The typewriter handles words; photography deals with still pictures; TV and cinema with moving pictures and sound; adding machines, calculators and computers manipulate numbers; . . . yet another endless list.

Each technology was designed primarily to meet the needs of a particular type of information. Advances in computing, microelectronics and telecommunications, however, have come together to form a unified electronic, digital, computer-based *information technology*. This enables all types of information to be handled using the same underlying principles.

In order to use this new technology efficiently and wisely, you need never 'go under the bonnet' to find out the intricate details of how the thing works, unless you are keen to delve further. This book assumes you want to know about the uses of the technology, not its inner techniques. Nevertheless, it is worth taking time to consider two fundamental principles and to get to know at least some of the technical jargon.

Principle numero uno of digital information technology goes like this: *All information can be represented as a code consisting of the digits 0 and 1; and all manipulations on that information can also be done using just 0s and 1s.*

You may think that this sounds too simplistic and/or too unbelievable to be of much use but many important scientific principles can be expressed in such simple terms and yet can have profound consequences.

The notion of using just two states (0 and 1) to represent information is not that outlandish when you consider that the full complexity and richness of the English language relies on just 26 characters plus a few punctuation marks. The Morse Code is a long-understood method of using two symbols to represent the alphabet and ten digits. This Code uses the sounds *dot* and *dash* as the basic *binary* code (binary means two, just as decimal means ten). Dot/dash, o/i, on/off are all examples of binary representations.

The second principle is the essence of computer-based systems: *The same pieces of equipment can be made to do different things by changing the program of instructions which automatically control the actions of the equipment; those programs can also be represented as os and is.*

Here come a few bits of essential jargon. Any physical piece of equipment is called *hardware*. *Programs* (not spelt 'programmes') are called *software*. You can see the hardware but the software controls the way you interact with the system. The fact that you can change software without changing hardware makes programmable information technology so versatile and so powerful. Chips of silicon (a constituent of sand) provide the hardware means of delivering that power here, there and everywhere. Information technology, too, is a many splendoured thing.

Everything with soft-centred chips

Electronics is an efficient and reliable way of representing a binary code. Thermionic valves, of the type onced used in radios, for example, could act as a switch where *on/off* could stand for o/i. Microelectronics is a way of shrinking such electronic switches into a tiny space. A thumbnail sliver of silicon could contain many thousands of such digits.

Silicon chips can therefore be used as a *memory* to *store* information as binary digits. They can also be used to hold and activate software programs; such chips are called *microprocessors* because the programs process information. These chip memories and microprocessors are so small and cheap that they can bring computing power to each desk.

You will not see the chips, unless you take the lid off some equipment. The most visible symbol of new electronic information technology in offices will be a TV-style screen and associated typewriter-style keyboard, often called a *VDU (Visual Display Unit)* or *VDT (Visual Display Terminal)*. Screens and keyboards are not only typical hardware components for a variety of office products, such as word processors and small desk-top computers, but can also provide links to large computers or other electronic devices.

Inside these units there are usually chips to store information and microprocessors that remember and operate programs. Other devices are also needed to print the results of processing and to store information and software in binary code.

Chips are also finding their way into traditional equipment. Inside telephones and telephone switchboards, for example, they provide enhanced services. Programmable switchboard exchanges offer increased efficiency and new aids for managing the way the telephone network is used.

These and many more examples of the application of programmable chips will be explored later in the book. New office technology will come in many different forms. Underneath them all, however, lurk the versatile chips and malleable software.

Everyone will be touched

Much of the public discussion about the electronic office has focused on secretaries, typists and clerks. These staff are important but are only part of the picture. They generally account for about 15% or less of all office staff costs.

The largest group of office employees are managers, administrators and professionals (scientists, engineers, accountants, planners, etc). Improving secretarial and clerical efficiency therefore can have a smaller impact on an organisation's costs than applying technology to aid managers and professionals.

The first wave of new office technology was spearheaded by the word processor, aimed at assisting typing activities. The next front is a mass army of products and services seeking out all other people and tasks in the office – without relenting on the word processing attack.

Computer-based systems will influence the lives of virtually everyone who does office work. The work sequences programmed into software will shape daily office routines. New ways of communicating, filing and finding information, performing calculations, analysing statistics, organising meetings and other activities using new technology will be a key factor in determining what jobs are available.

The range, pace and versatility of developments in information technology have been literally mind-boggling. Yet even the brightest technology should be subservient to the people who use it. The technology must be made to adapt to personal, social and organisational ways of doing things. If not, a technological dream could become a human nightmare, as Dr Frankenstein learnt to his cost.

What will happen to office jobs?

Office jobs are important to so many people that there has been much concern about how jobs may be altered by new technology – and whether the technology will be used to replace people. This has led to a great deal of speculation about whether more new jobs will be created than those destroyed by technology, something which can never be more than an imprecise numbers game.

Information technology is leading to so many changes throughout society and in all types of employment that no-one can predict with certainty the overall level of employment in the long term. There are, however, certain indisputable trends.

Change is inevitable. The jobs people do will change. New skills will have to be learnt. New job roles will emerge; old ones will fade, some disappear. One major reason for introducing new office technology into existing organisations is to enable fewer people to do more work. This will mean, in the short-term at least, a cut in the number of jobs at all levels in some organisations. On the other hand, technology will help to create new organisations and new jobs. These new jobs, however, could be in different geographical regions and industries, and may require different talents and training to traditional office work.

Organisations and the way they operate will change. New communications methods will open up new opportunities for managing people, teams, groups, departments, divisions, corporations.

Personnel policies will change: job gradings, pay rates and structures, training and retraining, career development, redeployment of staff, trade union bargaining, redundancy strategies, recruitment will adapt to the fluid changes in office jobs.

Office environments will change. Electronic technology will have to be accommodated and the health and comfort of staff re-assessed. New locations for office work will be made possible through the use of electronic devices linked by telecommunications channels. Such devices could be carried around in briefcases, based at the office worker's home or a local work centre, rather than in city centre office blocks.

Yes, there will be a lot of changes. A lot of things will also not change that much. As the French say, *Plus ça change, plus c'est la même chose*: the more things change, the more they stay the same. Technological innovation may proceed at a rapid pace, but people and organisations still assimilate change at their own slower and more natural pace.

Not To Be But How To Be: that is the question

Technological innovation in office work is inevitable; the technology is available at reasonable prices and offers so many obvious benefits that the electronic tide cannot be turned back now. *There is no inevitability, however, about how that technology will be applied within each organisation and to each task and job*. The software-centred nature of new office technology means that it should be possible to select and develop systems which closely match the way people wish to use them. There are limits in terms of technical feasibility and cost to what software can be made to do. Developing software can be time consuming and costly. Once software is installed, it can be difficult to alter. Nevertheless, the software capability means that the technology has a heart which can be made to beat in harmony with its users. New office technology is potentially versatile, adaptable and amenable to being tailor-made to fit each user's needs.

This introduction has outlined the major ideas needed to understand the nature of the technology and its impact on people and organisations. The rest of the book examines these ideas in more detail in terms of three key issues.

1 *The technology and what it does*. Chapter 1 looks at new office technology in some familiar surroundings. Chapter 2 describes how it is likely to be used in the future. Chapter 3 explains how the technology works, with more history and background (if you are interested) in Chapter 8. Future developments are outlined in Chapter 6. A dictionary of technical terms is provided in Chapter 9.

2 *How to control the technology*. Chapter 4 examines how new systems should be planned, designed, selected and run to ensure they meet real user requirements.

3 *Office jobs and what will happen to them*. Chapter 5 discusses the impact of new technology on office jobs and working routines.

Chapter 2 illustrates how a managing director, secretary and assistant manager may work in the future. Chapter 6 briefly looks at longer term possibilities.

As an additional helping hand, Chapter 7 provides a summary of practical advice given in the rest of the book by answering twenty key questions.

And now, for something not completely different

In your personal journey into the world of new office technology, you will meet many people eager to blind you with funny-sounding words. Salesmen, consultants and technical whizzkids love to sprinkle their chat with turgid technical terms and meaningless abbreviations. You should never feel intimidated by such jargon merchants. They should be made to explain to you *in terms you understand* why their technology is so marvellous.

Of course, you will have more confidence in battling your way through the jargon jungle if you understand the most important concepts and words. That is why this book will introduce you to some of that jargon. The term *software,* for example, was introduced early on because it is such an important idea that you will have little success unless you have it in your armoury. Just asking 'What kind of software is available?' is a giant step in getting to grips with the technologists.

As you find out what some of the strange words actually mean, you will realise that you are already familiar with equipment and services which have been given a smart new label. If you want an everyday example of *electronic mail*, you need look no further than the ordinary telephone or office telex. A company's automatic internal telephone switchboard may be called a *PABX* (Private Automatic Branch Exchange). Internal telephone links within a building are a form of what computer buffs call a *local area network.*

Electronic mail, PABXs and local area networks can have much wider scope and variety than the everyday versions, when boosted by the power of software and chips. The world of the electronic office should not be regarded as a strange land, completely different to everything you have known in the past. You will find much that is familiar and a development from traditional office methods.

Technology like the VDU may be the symbol of a new era in office work. The reason for doing office work is not, however, to offer a platform for technological fireworks. It is to provide a function or service that somebody wants or needs. Technology and technologists should not decide how changes occur. They should provide new options, new aids for office work. It will be people who understand what office work is trying to achieve who will decide how to make the best of the new capabilities.

The eventual story of the electronic office will unfold as people learn how to accommodate explosive technological innovations into new patterns of working and social life.

1   The electronic office in action

Take a look around town

Electronic office technology is not just a thing of the future. Many of the elements of the electronic office are already in widespread use and more are being installed every day.

The term 'electronic office' was probably first used in the early 1950s. In 1951 one of the world's first computers built for commercial office work became operational. It was developed by the British food company Lyons, famous for its corner tea shops. The system was called LEO, an abbreviation for Lyons' Electronic Office.

In the 1960s, more advanced computers than LEO were widely used to perform particular types of office work. They were large and expensive machines which had to be housed in special air conditioned rooms. They were therefore remote from the day to day life of people in offices, although office workers spent a lot of time gathering and preparing information for computers and sifting through the printed paper which spewed from them.

These early computers were particularly suited to tasks where there was a large volume of numerical information that needed to be processed quickly according to a clearly defined set of calculations. This is typical of the office work performed by accounts departments and in other financial activities.

Computers were therefore widely used to do things like calculating payrolls, printing pay slips, handling the calculations involved in preparing a company's accounts, producing customer bills (say, for telephones, gas and electricity), storing and updating customer accounts in banks, and many other important activities.

In the 1970s, computers began to spread their tentacles more directly into offices. The first VDUs were devices, known as *terminals*, which could be linked to a computer over telephone lines. From a terminal, someone in an office could make direct enquiries to the computer, update and feed new information to it and receive information from it.

It was then that the impact of the silicon chip began to be felt. As computing power became cheaper and more compact, it was brought closer to the work place. The chip brought computers into ordinary office environments.

Now, if you take a look around your local town, you will find many examples of electronic office systems in action. If you do office work, you will probably have come into direct contact with new technology at some stage. Everyone is likely to have come across the results of computer-aided office work in some aspect of their lives, often without being aware of the electronic connection.

So let us take a trip around town in search of new office technologies.

The shop on the corner

Our first stop is the shop on the corner to buy a packet of sweets, some fruit or a newspaper. Surprisingly, this shop could be the first electronic office on our trip.

The shop itself, of course, is not an office. In a backroom or upstairs, however, the shopkeeper will have somewhere to do the shop's paperwork. Most importantly, this includes keeping the accounts. A purchase ledger is used to record costs and purchases from suppliers and a sales ledger records the money taken from customers.

Accounts bookkeeping can now be done using a microcomputer with a suitable software package. After all, doing the accounts was one of the first commercial applications of the big old computers. once information is filed in binary code in some form of computer storage, other programs can be applied to it. For example, the sales figures could be analysed to detect any significant trends.

Other software on the same microcomputer can help the shopkeeper in a variety of ways. A newsagent, for example, can keep a computerised file of customers who get newspapers delivered or who have regular orders. Using a word processing program and the information in the customer file, the microcomputer can type routine reminders or produce a mail shot to all customers advising them of a new service.

The increasingly low cost of microcomputers puts them within reach of very small businesses and groups. Care should be taken, however, to ensure that the microcomputer has the ability to do what is required (the selection of systems is discussed in Chapter 4).

Inside an electronic wordsmithy

As we are on a technology hunt, it is important to sniff out businesses which have grown up with the technology, such as the word processing bureaux that have been popping up all over the place.

A typical bureau is a shop packed with word processors and printers. Typescript, handwritten information and voice tapes are brought in. The bureau then produces the required reports, letters, mail shots or other documents using its electronic systems.

A major advantage of a word processor is that it enables changes to the various drafts of a document to be made more efficiently than with a traditional typewriter. When a key is pushed, a mark is not made immediately on a piece of paper, as with a typewriter. Instead, the appropriate character is displayed on the word processor screen. At the same time it is recorded in digital code on computerised storage. Once the information has been transformed into electronic digital form, it can be manipulated automatically by software that allows the operator to delete, add to, alter and change the order of the text.

Word processors and associated equipment, like printers and computer storage media, require a substantial investment. Once a bureau has the equipment, it can then provide services to a variety of users whose individual needs might not justify their own systems.

Although word processors offer significant improvements in efficiency and flexibility, they are more effective in some activities than others. For example, word processors are better suited to a business which involves typing many long documents containing similar texts than one in which most typing consists of relatively short one-off letters.

There ain't no Sanity Clause

Legal documents are ideally suited to word processing. A solicitor's office should therefore be a good place to see a word processor earn its keep.

Legal documents are usually very wordy. The Marx Brothers film *A Night At The Opera* satirised such contracts, with Groucho and Chico tearing up one, clause by incomprehensible clause ('Party of the first part . . .,'). Finally, Groucho says, 'We are just left with the sanity clause. It is in every contract.' Chico retorts, 'You can't fool me. There ain't no Sanity Clause.'

Solicitors must take great care to ensure that any documents they produce comply precisely with the law. This leads to the inclusion of lots of standard clauses phrased in legal jargon. Many solicitors' documents contain a relatively small amount of information specific to a particular client, although the whole document may run to many pages.

With a word processor, standard clauses, paragraphs or whole documents can be kept permanently in encoded form on computer storage. A secretary or typist can then call up the appropriate text when required. This will be displayed on the screen for checking. It can be incorporated into the current document being produced, at the places indicated by the operator. Information specific to the client can be typed in where necessary. The blending of standard and specific text is done automatically. The word processor has many obvious benefits in this application. It cuts down the amount of text which has to be typed afresh for each document. This speeds up the typing process and cuts down on the likelihood of errors. Changes to the draft can similarly be made quickly and with relatively few errors.

This also illustrates some of the job changes created by new office technology. The solicitor's secretary or typist will need to learn how to operate the word processor. As this can eventually involve exploiting a wide range of computing capabilities, it can become a highly skilled job. On the other hand, less skill is required in producing the document.

Not only is a lot of the text produced automatically but word processing software can also handle the layout of the final printed report. Software can also be provided to check on spelling, so training in legal jargon could be less important.

For the business as a whole, the word processor could help cut costs, relieve the solicitors themselves of the tedious job of checking typing and allow more work to be handled by the same number (or fewer) people. As a result a solicitor may be able to expand business and offer an additional range of services to clients.

A peek through an office window

So far, we have looked at small businesses. A great deal of office work, of course, takes place in large public and private organisations and inside office blocks. So let us consider what the scene might be like in a typical departmental office of a big company or a local town council that is on the first rungs of the electronic office ladder.

The manager does not yet have any electronic equipment on the executive desk but her or his secretary does, although this is more likely to be an *electronic typewriter* than a word processor. An electronic typewriter is essentially a sophisticated automatic typewriter.

Electronic typewriters have much more limited computerised memory and software capabilities than word processors. They also do not have a screen; at most they have a single line display (strip window), typically of about 20 characters. Electronic typewriters however, are cheaper than word processors and can improve a typist's productivity significantly. A high percentage of typing errors, for example, are relatively trivial mistypings. With a single line display, the typist can spot and correct such errors before they are committed to paper.

Depending on the work of the office, there could be a number of screen/keyboard units around. If it is a sales department, there may be many clerks at VDUs typing in customer orders; such VDUs are likely to be terminals that can be linked to a computer somewhere else. The sales information can then be automatically processed by a central system that passes on the necessary details to accounts, production and other departments.

VDUs in customer service departments can be used to answer queries by being linked to computerised information libraries and to the company's main computer system. In a contracts department, word processors may be in evidence preparing the required contracts documents. An accounts department would probably have some microcomputers to assist with calculations and budget control; a few VDUs linked to the organisation's main computer; perhaps a word processor or two; and many calculators (which are the most common example, other than digital watches, of the way chips can be built into ordinary consumer products).

In many departments, the only visible evidence of the electronic office will be the telephone receivers. The telephone may have been around a long time but it is one of the most powerful avenues of communication to the electronic office.

Getting plugged into the wired office

From individual departments, let us pan out to a whole office building. When you walk into an office block, one of the first things you often see is a receptionist who doubles up as a switchboard operator. The telephone switchboard is the hub of a great deal of communications.

Suppose that the sales, customer service, contracts and accounting departments are in the same building. An automatic switchboard (PABX) enables internal calls to be dialled directly. PABXs could also be used to link up the word processors and microcomputers in the different departments.

This local area network can be used to exchange information, For example, a document typed on a word processor in the contracts department can be sent electronically to word processors in the sales and accounts departments, where they can either be printed out or checked on the screen. Shorter messages may also be sent by such *electronic mail* between word processors, microcomputers and VDUs.

Of course, the telephone can also be used – but this is a typical scene:

The sales manager tries to phone the contracts manager. The number is engaged. Ten minutes later it is still engaged. Half-an-hour later, the sales manager gets through to the contracts manager's secretary: 'He's somewhere in the building but I don't know where. I'll leave a message for him.'

Quarter-of-an-hour later, the contracts manager returns. The secretary is out and has forgotten to leave a message. She returns but the manager has gone out again. An hour later the manager returns. 'Could you phone the sales manager,' says the secretary. The contracts manager tries – but the line is engaged; tries again in ten minutes – still engaged; goes off to a meeting.

Meanwhile, the sales manager has rushed off to a potential customer, fuming at the contracts manager for not providing some vital information. The sales manager loses the customer's business because of the lack of that information. Next morning, the contracts manager phones the sales manager. Gets through. '**** !!!,' swears the sales manager. '!!!! ***,' swears back the contracts manager.

With new forms of electronic mail, things can be different. Back on day one, the sales manager could have typed a message (or, on some systems, spoken it) once it was known that the contracts manager was unavailable. The message would have been sent to the contract manager's terminal, where it would have been stored, ready to be looked at as soon as the manager came into the room.

A reply could be prepared and sent immediately to the sales manager. Armed with this information, the sales manager might have won the business.

Efficient means of local area network communications are available other than using a PABX as the hub.

Long distance information

Of course, people also need to communicate between office blocks, not only within the same building. Traditionally, the post and telephone have been the most popular forms of communications across long distances. Other methods of telecommunication have also been available for a long time.

It is quite likely that, lurking somewhere in an office building there is a telex room. Telex is essentially a teleprinter service. In the early 1980s there were well over 1 million telex subscribers around the world. The sales department, for example, can use telex to communicate with staff in other countries. Though not the fastest of methods, it is particularly useful when a printed copy of the information is needed, as in the following example.

The sales manager receives an urgent request from a salesman in a faraway place for details of a new products. The manager gives the information to a secretary to take to the telex room. The secretary arrives at the room to find she is in a queue. At the front of the queue is someone sending a really long report. So the secretary fills in a few forms and leaves the information with the telex controller.

Sometime later, the telex operator types the information on a telex unit, which looks like a cumbersome typewriter. Each telex has an address code, equivalent to a phone number. The message being typed is sent to the appropriate telex number of the place where the salesman is waiting for the information.

At the other end, the message is printed out automatically on a teleprinter. Although he is pleased to get the information, he frowns when he gets the message. It is full of product codes and prices that have been printed a bit messily, in capital letters with lots of misspellings, punctuation (like STOP) spelt out and with control messages sent between telex operators.

The salesman eventually makes sense of most of the message but needs some more information, so telexes back to headquarters. When the message arrives, it has to be delivered from the telex room, which causes a delay, waiting for the internal messenger to return from another delivery.

Eventually, the sales manager gets the telex. The extra information involves the sending of some diagrams and pictures of products. Telex is no good for this but luckily the company has *facsimile* transmission (more chummily known as *fax*).

Making copies down the line

Fax is a *telecopier*. There needs to be a fax machine at each end of a telecommunications link, one switched to 'send', one to 'receive'. When the sales manager sends ten pages down to the fax room, the fax operator dials the number of the fax receiver using an ordinary telephone and establishes that the receiving end is ready. A page is then inserted in the sending fax as it might be in a photocopier. At the other end of the line, a copy is made on the receiving device.

Each page takes a few minutes to send to the agent. What with the setting up time and other delays, the salesman has a frustrating wait of over half-an-hour. When the copies arrive, they are a bit fuzzy and some of the diagrams have to be redrawn before being presented to the client. Nevertheless, ten hazy copies in hand is better than perfect originals in the post.

Telex and fax are well established forms of electronic mail, providing useful services. They have been held back, however, by the practical disadvantages described in the examples – slowness, poor quality, and so on. Fax machines from different manufacturers often cannot communicate with each other, which is one reason why fax has been relatively unpopular, with three times fewer users than telex in 1980.

Software and chips have given fax and telex a new lease of digital life. Telex terminals can now have screens. Software enables messages to be laid out properly. New printers provide faster, better quality message printing. A 'super-telex' (*teletex*) international standard allows word processors to link into the old telex network. (Teletex is not to be confused with *teletext*, an information service that can be broadcast to specially adapted TV sets).

Fax machines have become digitised and use software techniques to be quicker (a page can be telecopied in less than 30 seconds) and to give better quality than traditional facsimile devices.

Another sleeping electronic beauty

While pondering on older technologies revitalised by a kiss from an electronic prince, we shouldn't overlook the dear old telephone. Like a granny in a mini skirt with a punk hairdo, even the telephone is being updated. PABXs are becoming computer controlled and chips are finding their way into telephone handsets. To see the effect, we need to look into an office which has a few of these new gadgets. In this office, a manager is sitting in front of a push button phone, which has a few more buttons than usual. She picks up the receiver, pushes one button, continues writing a memo, then starts talking. She has used the *auto-dial* facility. Regularly used numbers are stored in the telephone's chip memory and are activated by a code consisting of just one or two digits. The number is dialled automatically.

Meanwhile, another manager has picked up a phone and used an auto-dial number in a similar way. He finds the number is engaged. So he presses a button and replaces the receiver, then carries on working. A few minutes later, his phone rings. He picks it up and speaks. He has just used a *repeat dial* capability, which automatically re-dials an engaged number until it is free.

Both the managers finish their calls, push a few more buttons, then leave the room to have a private meeting in a separate room. They have programmed their PABX to re-route calls automatically from their usual office extensions to the telephones in their meeting room.

They have gone to discuss a report produced by PABX software. This analyses the department's use of the telephone. It identifies the total costs, how much of this was for local and how much for long distance and foreign calls, whether calls were made in peak-cost periods, and so on.

The system does not record the content of telephone conversations but it can identify and report where calls are made to from each extension.

From this report, the managers identify that a lot of peak-time international calls had been made from a particular extension, so they decide to talk to that group to find out why. They find other areas where they need to ask questions in order to bring down costs – including why so many 'dial-a-disc' calls were made from an extension close to where a couple of young clerks work.

Since getting this analysis, soaring telephone costs have been controlled. They can isolate any trouble spots and sort them out. Staff have become aware that their own usage can be pinpointed and are more careful. In the past, all telephone costs had been bundled together and requests to use the telephone more efficiently had been ignored because specific problems could not be identified.

Money through the wall

Having spent a lot of time in and around office buildings, it is time to step back into the outside world. Before going to do a bit of shopping, let us go to the bank to get some money.

Most people have stood in a queue at a bank waiting to cash a cheque while someone at the front seems to spend an eternity paying in sacks of money. This still happens but many banks have now installed automatic cash dispensers. So now you find yourself standing in a queue to get at the cash dispenser while someone at the front takes ages fiddling with the machine trying to get it to work.

Cash dispensers placed on the wall outside banks provide access to money when the bank is closed. Their operation should be simple, although some equipment has been badly designed or is placed in poorly lit surroudings so that it can seem complicated to a newcomer.

Instead of a cheque on which you write the amount you want and provide your signature for verification, you need only a plastic card and a *Personal Identification Number* (*PIN*). On the plastic card is a strip of magnetically-coated material which holds some computerised digits, such as your PIN password.

You put the plastic card in the cash dispenser. On a display, it asks you for your number. You type it on a keypad built into the machine. If you make a mistake, you get a couple of chances to get it right; then it will put a block on further tries in case the card has been stolen. Once you give it the right PIN, it asks how much you want. You key in a number; wait a few seconds; then the crisp notes come sliding out.

In many cases, the dispenser is a terminal linked directly to the bank's central computers containing your account. In the twinkling of an eye, a message is sent via a telecommunications link to check your bank balance to make sure you have enough to cover your request and your account is debited automatically.

Electronic cash catches on

As we want to know what is happening to office work, let us step into the bank and go behind the front-office scenes. As mentioned at the start of this chapter, banks were amongst the first major users of computers in the early 1960s. Banking and other finance-based businesses have also been major growth areas in office work.

Money is the most vivid example of the value of information. A cash note is basically a worthless bit of paper. So is a cheque. What gives them value is the information printed in and on the note or the writing and signature on the cheque. It is therefore not a startling leap to think of money in the form of electronic signals in digital codes, which is another form of information representation.

Most bank accounts are now stored on a computer. This makes it possible to have automatic tellers and cash dispensers. Even the most elementary cash dispenser clearly cuts down on office work that would have otherwise been done by staff handling a cheque.

Banks' computers can also exchange information with each other. You could ask your bank, for example, to pay a store a standing order, which automatically transfers the same amount each month from your account to the computer containing the store's account. A direct debit could be programmed into your computerised account to pay your mortgage or some other regular payment where the amount could vary. Standing orders and direct debits can even be set up, changed and cancelled from some automatic tellers.

There was a time when most people got paid in cash. Now, more and more people get salaries paid directly into their bank's account, by transferring information from a computer containing the employer's bank account to those of the employees.

Such electronic cash transactions, called *Electronic Funds Transfer Systems (EFTS)*, open the way for great reductions in paperwork and, therefore, office work carried out by people. The majority of mail consists of financial transactions – bills, invoices, statements, cheques. With greater use of word processors and other electronic mail, together with banks' computers, many of these transactions could take place in purely electronic form.

Behind the solid exterior of your local bank, office work is in a state of bubbling change.

Computing links in supermarket chains

After getting some money from the bank, you may think of going to a supermarket. Let us suppose that it is the local branch of a large chain of stores. Probably the only electronic device visible to you is the checkout till; or there may be an electronic weighing machine that automatically prints out labels with prices of the fruit and veg weighed on it.

As with the bank, the real impact of computing goes on behind the scenes. There is a whole network of suppliers, manu-facturers, warehouses, distribution centres, and so on which ensure that the store gets the right goods at the right time. Perishables like fruit, meat and dairy products must be kept fresh, so the store must ensure it does not order too much. Deliveries of fresh goods must be prompt.

Keeping all these links in the supermarket chain operating smoothly involves the handling of a lot of information. Details of sales must be recorded both for accounting and to help managers identify trends. A record must be kept of all the goods ordered, their arrival at the shop, the goods held in the shop's store and stock on the shelves.

Such inventory control must ensure that there are not too many goods in stock. That would cost a lot and some of the goods would go stale or become outdated. On the other hand, if stocks are too low, customers will be unhappy if they cannot get what they want. Efficient stock control relies on the quick gathering, updating and analysing of information.

Your local supermarket may be one of many hundreds in the chain. Information needs to be gathered from all these and fed to the group's distribution centres, warehouses, suppliers and factories. All this information has led to a great deal of office work. Much of it, however, can now be done electronically.

The electronic check-out till, for example, can do much more than just add up your bill and tell the assistant how much change to give. It can be a fully fledged computer-based *PoS terminal* (PoS in an abbreviation for Point of Sale which, in a supermarket, is the checkout.)

A PoS terminal can gather information on sales and feed it to a central computer linked to all the checkouts in the store. This would enable sales statistics to be analysed quickly while also monitoring the performance of each checkout cashier.

You could pay for goods with a plastic card, similar to the one needed for an automatic cash dispenser. The PoS terminal can have an attachment to deal with the card and can be linked directly to your bank account.

Stock control is a classic computing application dating back to the 1960s. Invoices, bills and payments can be handled electronically through EFTS systems. Word processors, micro-computers, electronic mail and other computerised services can be used to fill most of the other information links.

Time for a holiday

Coming out of the supermarket, your eye catches a display in the window of a travel agent. You go in to see what other tempting holidays are on offer. When you walk into the shop, you notice there is a TV set near the counter. It is not showing moving pictures but a screenful of information.

This is an example of *videotex*, more commonly known as *view-data*. It is like an electronic library containing lots and lots of pages of information. Travel agents use viewdata a lot to be kept informed of the availability of holidays, flights and so on.

The pages in the electronic viewdata library are held in computer storage and can be updated from terminals, so they can be up-to-the-minute. In some countries there are public viewdata services which you can get on an ordinary home TV set with a special adaptor. Public viewdata has a wider variety of information than specialised systems, such as those used by travel agents.

Having chosen a flight to somewhere sunny, the next task is to book an airline ticket. Together with banks, airlines were pioneer users of computers in the 1960s. They were the first to introduce terminals linked to computers into their everyday business.

Air travellers frequently make flights involving more than one airline for different legs of the journey. They also change their mind and want to switch flights. Only by having computerised systems, with reservation staff linked by terminal to the latest information, is it possible for airlines to handle the huge amount of information that needs to be sorted out so quickly.

The travel agent typically phones up the airline or holiday company. At the other end of the line is a clerk with a terminal. New electronic systems like viewdata enable the agents to do their own electronic searches of information and to make reservations direct from a terminal in their own office.

New fashions in design

As we walk around town, you notice a few building sites. Although the completed buildings may be used for offices, you may think nothing could be further away from office work than the bashing, bricking and heaving that goes on when putting up a new building.

You would be wrong however. The site manager has a lot of office work to do in keeping track of the progress on the project, the costs, materials being used, hours worked and payments to staff, and so on. It is quite likely that, on the bigger sites at least, there is a microcomputer in the site manager's hut helping with this office work.

Every building must have an architectural design on which it is based. If we step into an architect's office, we may find an electronic device different to the ones we have been discussing so far.

Much architectural work deals with the sketches and detailed drawings of a building's design. Most of the other devices we have looked at are ideal for dealing with words and numbers.

The architect would therefore need a special *graphics* terminal suited to assisting with design work.

A graphics terminal comes with an electronic pen, called a *light pen*. With this, the architect can 'draw' images on a screen, which are also fed into computer store. These can then be manipulated, turned into three-dimensional perspective, viewed from various angles, rotated, and so on.

Once a design has been agreed, a lot of work in an architect's office is carried out by draughtsmen who create the detailed drawing to be used by the builders. Computers can do a lot of this work using devices such as a *plotter* which can draw lines under software direction.

Graphics terminals, plotters, suitable software and other devices combine to form Computer Aided Design (CAD) systems. These can be applied to office work done in many other areas of design, such as new product engineering (car manufacturers use CAD extensively) and clothes design.

Dealing with dealers

Continuing on our way, you decide to visit a car dealer to get something for your car. The dealer tells you he has not got what you want in stock but he will find out from the manufacturer when he can get you one. He then makes a strange telephone call.

He picks up the receiver and uses a push button keypad to dial a number. You hear a voice answering him at the other end. But instead of speaking back, he keys in some more numbers. This 'conversation' goes on for a bit. The dealer then tells you that he can get you a yellow one (of what ever you asked for) in two weeks or a red one in six weeks. You say you are prepared to wait for the red one. He keys in some more numbers then you hear the voice on the phone say 'Goodbye'.

You have witnessed what is called a *voice response* computer system. The voice on the other end of the line was not a person. An actor had recorded a lot of words and phrases. This recording was then translated into digital code and stored in the car manufacturer's computer, which is linked to the dealer network.

The dealer dials a number that connects him to the central computer, which has details of parts and product availability. If the dealer had a VDU, the computer would have replied with a message on a screen. Instead, it puts together the pre-recorded words so that the response sounds as if it were a live person at the end of the line.

The computer checks on stocks, informs the dealer of avail-abilities and delivery times. It can also answer a lot of other questions. When the dealer places the order for what you want, the computer automatically updates its files to keep the relevant production, distribution and accounting departments informed.

This automatic processing of orders takes over a lot of office work that would previously have been done by clerks at the manufacturer's. A clerk would have had to answer the phone from the dealer, take time to check on the order availability, then write down the details of the order. This information would then have to be prepared and passed on to other departments.

The traditional form of clerical work was error prone and took so much time that the information given to the dealer over the phone could be well out of date. This would eventually mean that you might not get your part when you expected it. The electronic system should be more efficient and reliable.

Matchmaker, matchmaker find me a job

So far, we have looked at people in jobs using new technology. There are, of course, many people who do not have jobs. For them, a walk around town can be a depressing experience, with the public job centre and private employment bureaux as the focal points in their search for a job.

Matching people to job vacancies is, in fact, a classic task carried out by computers. The kinds of card file kept on applicants and vacancies can be easily computerised. The process of 'matchmaking' is one which computers frequently do, whether it is matching lonely hearts in computer dating operations, helping people to find jobs or a home, or in any other way searching through a file trying to find factors that match certain criteria.

If you go to a job centre, the person interviewing you is likely to write your name, address, phone number, qualifications, skills, experience, special needs, etc on a card. This card may be filed in alphabetical order with other job applicants. The centre will also have files with details of employers and jobs available.

There are many ways in which the card files may be searched. The centre's staff, for example, may wish to find an employer's or applicant's address; or to look for jobs in an area; or to seek jobs with particular skills requirements; or to get a list of jobs in a certain age range.

This can be awkward with a physical card index. With a computer system, however, an electronic file equivalent of the card index can be created. Each card can be presented on a VDU screen if required. It is much quicker and easier for staff to search through these files and to get lists of appropriate jobs or applicants.

The centre's staff tells the software controlling the file search which key factors are wanted. For example: 'all applicants over 25 with a driving licence and at least one year's experience in selling,' or, 'all applicants between 16 and 19 living locally and with a basic qualification in English and Mathematics.' The software automatically searches through the computerised file, finds the appropriate records, presents them on the screen when requested and, if necessary, prints out a list of suitable applicants.

Once such information is in digital form, the centre can use word processing software to extract the name and address from the file for use in writing letters to employers and applicants.

Such computerised systems usually require that the information is supplied in concise form and works best on factors which can be expressed crisply and unambiguously, like exam qualifications, age, length of experience in particular skills, etc. Some of the information about an applicant, however, is more generalised, such as reasons for being unemployed, the applicant's hopes and expectations, special family circumstances, the employer's traditions, and so on.

The computer system can therefore help to speed up the job search. Discretion must still, however, be allowed to staff at the centre both to advise employers and to select applicants based on a broader understanding of the issues involved than can be placed on the computer files and handled by the software.

To serve us all our days

Office work can provide a vital service in helping to care for people, from birth to death.

The kinds of electronic office aids described earlier can be used in a variety of public services, for example, helping to process information and produce cheques to pay pensions, welfare and unemployment benefits. In your local doctor's or dentist's surgery, school, hospital, adult education centre, or city council, the electronic office can help to make administration quicker, more efficient and more responsive.

Microcomputers can be used to handle patients' files, automatically send reminders to parents about vaccinations, and otherwise assist doctors and dentists. Bigger computers are usually used in government departments dealing with, say, welfare payments because of the large volume of information involved. Local offices of these departments, can use smaller computers and terminals to assist in dealing with their clients.

Local councils are likely to have a mix of large and small computers, word processors, telex, graphics terminals and fax because they are large organisations covering a wide variety of activities and locations.

There are also many local community groups and voluntary agencies who can make valuable use of electronic office systems. Much of the office work of such groups consists of maintaining files of members, sending out regular notices to them, and producing reports and letters. A microcomputer with suitable file handling software, a word processing package and adequate printer can help the many volunteers in these groups get to the heart of the issues they are concerned about.

Using a phone box as an office

As we return home after our electronic-office-spotting tour, we notice one last example: a phone box on the corner of the street. Surely, you might think, there is no way that a phone box can be thought of as an office. It is only in Dr Who's science fiction Tardis that a phone booth expands when you enter it.

Of course, it is not the booth which is meant to double as an office. The important thing is that the booth contains a telephone. In the world of electronic information, a telephone is as much a gateway to computing power as is a three-point plug and socket to electricity power.

Portable computers and terminals are now available which can be carried around in a briefcase. If you are a travelling salesman who needs to send back details of orders each day, in dire straits you may use a call box as a way of connecting your terminal to your company's computer rather than from your home or a hotel room.

You can also use the call box to send electronic mail or check the contents of your own electronic mailbox, if your company has such a system. You can use your terminal/computer to prepare letters and reports while on a plane or train journey, then use a call box to whizz the information back to your office.

There seems to be no escaping the electronic office.

The future began yesterday

This chapter has shown that the world of the electronic office is not far away. It has already arrived. In many cases, it has come quietly and almost unnoticed. At times, it has been accompanied by razzmatazz and coverage on TV, radio and in the press.

On occasions, the introduction of new office technology has led to strikes and disruption of work. As can be seen from the examples in this chapter, new technology changes the nature of jobs and threatens the existence of many. This naturally leads to fear amongst staff. In organisations with poor labour relations, this can erupt into opposition to new technology.

Despite such problems, which are discussed in more detail later in the book, the main elements in the electronic office have been taking their place in everyday working life. The examples given in this chapter are just a small fraction of what is going on.

By keeping a look-out in your own daily life, you will find many more illustrations of electronic office systems in action. There are also many products in everyday use which use the same software-and-chips principles; digital watches, electronic cookers, electronic games, are just a few.

In the next chapter we will look a little more into the future to see what work might be like when the various elements that comprise the electronic office are brought together and are in widespread use.

2 A day in electronic office life

A trip to tomorrow's world

The previous chapter showed how part of today's office work is being carried out by new office technology. This usage is patchy, and progress often takes place in a higgledy-piggledy way. Given current trends, however, eventually most office work will be carried out the electronic way.

What will office life be like then? This chapter sketches out what might one day be an ordinary working day for three typical office workers – a managing director of a small company; a secretary working in a large company; and an assistant manager in the department of a local government authority.

As well as giving an idea of what could occur in the electronic office, this chapter will continue the process of introducing and describing electronic office equipment and services, to help you expand your own armoury of technical jargon.

Without stepping outside the front door

Our tomorrow's world managing director gets up bright and not so early. As she is working from home today, she doesn't need to spend any time commuting to work. When the alarm goes, she can turn over for just ten minutes more dreamy sleep.

After breakfast, her husband, a social worker, takes the children to school. While finishing her coffee in the sitting room, the managing director turns on the TV to get in touch with her bank. Her house is wired-in to a cable network that not only provides 30 TV channels but also offers new tele-services, like *telebanking*.

The managing director picks up a remote control keypad. This can be used to switch channels and turn the volume up or down. It can also be used to send information to a remote computer, just as if it were a VDU, with the TV screen as the display and the keypad as the keyboard.

She switches the TV channel selector to the telebanking service and instructs it, via the keypad, to connect her to her own bank's computer. Once she is linked directly *online* to her bank, she engages in an *interactive* dialogue with the system. As her keypad only has digits rather than a full typewriter keyboard, this dialogue is similar to that used in many viewdata services, such as the travel agent system discussed in the previous chapter. The computer presents a menu with a list of options. As in a Chinese restaurant, there is a number against each item. Key in the number and you activate the associated item on the menu.

Before being allowed to do anything, the managing director has to key in a personal password, just as you have to do with an automatic cash dispenser. Once she has done this and indicated that she wishes to access the family's current account, the system presents a menu, such as:

o – check balance
1 – make payment transfer
2 – change standing orders
3 – request overdraft allowance
.
.
.

She first keys in 'o'. Her current balance is shown on the screen. She then keys '1'. She authorises a payment transfer to the local council to pay her rates. She then enquires about a short-term overdraft. The computer automatically checks her past record and assets. It responds by saying she can overdraw to half the amount she asked for. If she needs more she must make a personal visit to her bank manager.

Having done her banking for the day, the managing director switches off the television. In ten minutes, over coffee in the comfort of her home, she has done some useful private work which might otherwise have involved an uncomfortable and time wasting visit to the bank. The bank has also saved itself a lot of managerial and clerical effort.

The managing director now walks to her office, a room in her house. Without stepping outside her front door, she is about to do a full day's work.

An office is where a workstation is

The managing director is working from home today because her company is at a critical point in the development of a new product, a microprocessor controlled Thingamajig. She needs to make some crucial decisions to overcome a development snag and to get the sales and marketing programme underway.

She works from home a couple of days a week on average. To help her, she has a versatile *workstation* in her office at home. A few of the other senior managers have similar systems at home and others rely on portable workstations – microcomputers and terminals that can be carried in a briefcase.

'Workstation' is an all-purpose word to identify the place and device from which work is carried out. A word processor is a workstation. A microcomputer is a workstation. Come to think of it, an old fashioned desk, typewriter and telephone could be called a workstation.

The workstation in the managing director's home is a cross between a *personal computer* (a general name given to a micro-computer used primarily for personal tasks) and a VDU terminal used to communicate with other workstations and the company's main computer. It has some features worth lingering on.

The screen has black characters on a white background; this is know as *positive presentation*. Other screens usually have a light character (such as white, green or orange) on a darker back-ground (black, greyish or brown). Colour displays provide multi-colour presentations. When a domestic TV is used as the display, say with a home microcomputer or in a service like telebanking or viewdata, the colour TV will produce multi-colour displays, of a lower quality than VDU screens.

The screen on the managing director's workstation does not just consist of lines of text, as would a typical word processor. A VDU screen can be considered as a 'window' onto the store of computerised information to which it is connected. Initial elec-tronic systems allowed for just a single window. The type of system used by the managing director has *multiple windows* (also known as *split screen*).

While the managing director is working on one document, other pages or documents can be shown in other windows. She can switch from the window on which she is currently working to do other work through another window.

A multiple window display makes the screen act in a similar way to an ordinary desk top on which one could spread a few documents.

Of mice and ikons

The managing director also has an electronic mouse on her desk. A *mouse* is a small device that can be moved around the surface of the desk. The movement of the mouse influences the movement of a pointer on the screen. This pointer, called a *cursor,* identifies the place where the user is currently operating.

With a word processor or microcomputer, the cursor is usually moved by special cursor control keys which move it up, down, left and right. A mouse-controlled cursor can be used to point to images on the screen. A word processor's cursor shows where the next character is to be inserted, which word is to be deleted, and so on.

The managing director's screen displays little diagrams, called *ikons*, that symbolise filing cabinets and folders, a calculator, and other functions carried out by the computer. When the managing director wishes to look through her computerised file, she uses the mouse to position the cursor over the ikon representing a file. She presses a button on the mouse, which activates the file handling software.

She can also call up the calculator function. This displays a drawing on the screen that looks like a calculator. By moving the mouse, the cursor can be moved over the 'keys' on the screen calculator and it will perform just as if it were a calculator. The managing director, however, rarely uses this feature. She finds moving the mouse too fiddly for this purpose and still relies on a trusty old calculator which she keeps in her desk drawer.

Of course, the managing director's workstation also has a keyboard which can be used to enable the workstation to perform the functions of a word processor, microcomputer or terminal.

And so to work

The first thing the managing director does is to see what is in her electronic mailbox. This is stored on computer files located at the company's headquarters. So she keys in the appropriate 'telephone number' on the push button phone on her desk. This connects her through the public telephone network to the local area network at her headquarters and therefore to all the electronic office systems, workstations and storage at HQ.

She has to *log in* before she can do anything with the information in her computerised files. She does this by keying in her password. The computer recognises the code and identifies that it is coming from the managing director's home terminal.

This security check is vital. Once the lock has been opened, the managing director can look through and change her own files. As she is managing director, her personal password also indicates to the computer that she has special privileges to look through departmental and other company files, although other executives have their private files that nobody else can get at.

The first thing the managing director does is to review what is in the 'in tray' of her electronic mail box. A summary is given on the screen of the messages stored in computer memory waiting to be forward to her workstation (that is why this type of electronic mail capability is called *store and forward*.) This summary gives a brief idea of the subject matter of each item of electronic mail, who sent it, what time it arrived, and its level of urgency.

For the moment, the managing director is interested only in messages relating to the Thingamajig project, so she looks at each of these in more detail. Two important memos have come from overseas agents, who work in countries with a 5-hour and 8-hour time difference from hers. In the past, this meant a lot of phone calls at unsocial hours. Using electronic mail, international communication is much more convenient because messages are sent and received at convenient times for all parties.

Confirm – to avoid disputes

In addition to the Thingamajig messages, the managing director also deals with a message from the personnel director that had been highlighted as urgent. This asks the managing director to agree to a salary for a new job in the marketing department. It is urgent because an interviewee is due in at 10 a.m.

The managing director adds (*appends* is the jargon word) her own electronic note to the personnel manager's memo. She immediately instructs the system to return the original memo and her appended reply to the personnel manager, with a copy to the marketing manager.

The managing director indicates that the message has '*immediate*' top priority status. She instructs the system to put a control on the message that means it can be read by the personnel and marketing managers only after they have confirmed that they have received the message. This avoids any subsequent dispute about whether or not her message had been received on time.

Once she has prepared her message, she presses a SEND key on her workstation. The reply then awaits in her electronic 'out tray'. *Network control* software which runs the electronic mail system regularly checks such out trays. The 'immediate' status means that the managing director's message is transferred immediately to the recipients' electronic 'in trays'.

Other degrees of urgency could have been specified. For

example, an 'overnight' status would mean that the network control software waited until a period when it had relatively little else to do before transferring the message.

Decisions, decisions . . . all the time decisions

British cartoonist Frank Dickens once showed his harassed office manager Bristow being approached by the tea lady. He beams as he takes the tea. 'One sugar lump or two, love,' she asks. Bristow collapses in tears. 'Decisions, decisions . . . all the time decisions,' he moans.

The most important aspect of any managerial job is to make decisions. The electronic office provides a variety of aids, called by the general term *Decision Support Systems* (*DSS*). For the managing director, there are two such aids which she finds particularly useful: receiving accurate information at her fingertips; and help in predicting the likely course of events, depending on the decision she chooses.

The first things she wants to do is review her Thingamajig file. So she positions the cursor over a file ikon to indicate she wishes to look through the product development folder in her Thingamajig file. On the screen she scans through some recent memos from the product development manager. The problem is clearly related to a Blue Widget.

The company maintains a widget *database* service. A database is a large collection of computerised information organised and managed by *Data Base Management Software* (*DBMS*). Information organised as in traditional filing, with separate files for each activity, is known as a *file management* system. A database run under full DBMS control is more flexible, accurate and efficient.

The Widget database allows the manager to ask various questions about the progress of research and development into widgets in general and the Blue Widget in particular. It also includes summaries of news and research information relating to the world of widgets outside her company. She looks at this widget database through one window on the screen while keeping a window on her own file at the same time.

Much of her morning is taken up gathering information, including the exchange of some electronic mail messages with the Thingamajig project team. The speed and ease of getting information, the comfort of her surroundings and the lack of constant interruptions (she deals with electronic mail messages when she is ready for them), gives her lots of that precious commodity – time to think.

Doubts about electronic diaries

Using the information she has gathered and analysed, the managing director makes some decisions about what might be going wrong with the Blue Widget. She sends electronic messages to get tests underway to check her theories. She also fixes a meeting with the Thingamajig project manager using the electronic diary capability on the information network. Each manager's diary is stored within the system so that meetings can be arranged through them automatically.

Some managers have complained that they don't like having their days arranged like this; some have taken to making up fictitious appointments to keep control over at least part of their day. A few managers have also complained that electronic mail, with its ability to monitor the times of messages, their content and whether they are received, inhibits the free flow of information and puts them under pressure by making them feel they are being monitored.

The managing director has employed a consultant to investigate the way such electronic office systems affect the behaviour of managers and to recommend if changes should be made.

Getting personal

For the afternoon, the managing director concentrates on working out a sales and marketing budget for the Thingamajig. For this, she uses her workstation as a personal computer running one of the most popular forms of decision support system, the *electronic spreadsheet*.

She has her own copies of the spreadsheet software and her budget files. These are held on *floppy disks*, which resemble flexible 45 rpm music discs (because of the strong American influence on computing, computer 'disks' is spelt with a 'k'). Information is stored in the magnetic coating on the disk. The disk is kept permanently in a cover to protect it from dirt; the cover has a hole in it through which a *read/write head* (equivalent to the needle of a record player) can get at the information on the floppy disk.

The managing director places the floppy disk with the spreadsheet software into a *disk drive*. This is the unit containing the read/write head and with a slot into which the disk in its jacket is slipped. It reads the program into the memory of the workstation. As the manager does not want to overwrite this program, the floppy disk is protected from being written to, just as you can guard a music cassette tape against being over-recorded.

What would happen if . . .?

The spreadsheet program presents a grid of lines on the screen that can represent a series of rows and columns. The managing director has already set up a file for a Thingamajig sales and marketing spreadsheet. She loads this floppy disk file into a second disk drive on the workstation. This saves her keying in all the information again, which would be a laborious task.

The rows and columns in this spreadsheet have been allocated to factors such as expected sales volume for the Thingamajig; wholesale price; expected retail price; discount to be given for bulk purchase; number of sales staff; commission to be given to staff; staff salaries; expected total staff costs; total income expected in the first year; expected profits/losses, etc.

When she first set up this spreadsheet, the managing director also specified mathematical rules linking the various factors. For example, 'sales price × sales volume = total income'. More complex rules were also built in.

When she alters one element in the spreadsheet, all others linked to it by one of these rules are also changed, according to the relevant formula. This enables her to ask a lot of *What if . . .?* questions. 'What if we increase commission to sales staff by 5%, reduce discount for bulk supply by 2.5% and increase the sales price by 1% to cover any extra Blue Widget cost?' is one of many options she can ask her software, after putting it into a concise form understood by the program.

The spreadsheet program is an example of *modelling* and *simulation* techniques widely used to assist decision makers. The rules defined by the software create a 'model' that simulates the way a financial system operates, in a similar way to which a Computer Aided Design system models a building according physical laws programmed into the software. Larger computers are needed to run modelling software that handles more information, more factors to be considered and more sophisticated rules than is possible on a small system. The managing director can use more powerful systems by linking up to the company's main computer.

She also likes to use graphics software to create graphs and diagrams from the computer's facts and statistics. Graphics are much easier to interpret than a load of numbers.

You may sometimes stand alone

With the aid of the spreadsheet program, the managing director decides what she believes is a reasonable budget for the selling and marketing of Thingamajig. She now wants to prepare a report, so she reads a word processing program from disk to replace the spreadsheet software in the computer's memory. She also places a new floppy disk in the second drive to store the report.

While working on the spreadsheet model and using the word processing package to write her memo, the managing director has her workstation in *stand-alone* mode, running completely off its own computing power. As a terminal, it uses costly communications links and adds to the demand on the already overworked central computers handling the network.

She has the best of both worlds. The workstation can be used for personal work and then linked to the corporate system. When operating *offline* as a stand-alone device, it can be used to prepare the report without tying up communications and computing resources while she slowly types it in and then corrects and revises it.

Once the report is ready on disk, she switches the workstation back to being a terminal and whooshes the report through the electronic mail system to the five people who must comment on it. Her day's work is done.

The managing director takes a final check on her electronic mailbox. Sees there is nothing urgent. Closes the office door. And Hey Presto! she is home again.

Why the secretary is half-an-hour late

Our second snapshot of the electronic office is of a secretary working for a large multinational company. In fact, her job title is not 'secretary' or 'personal assistant' but 'Manager, Executive Support Group'. She reports directly to the manager of the marketing department and is in charge of a group of five secretaries and word processing operators who work for about 20 sales executives in the department. For convenience, we will still call her 'the secretary.'

She arrives half-an-hour late for work because she has been to an optician, paid for by the company. As part of a *technology agreement* between the management and unions, all staff who work with word processors or VDUs are given frequent eye tests.

Using screen-based word processors or VDUs can cause eyestrain, so regular check-ups and adjustments in spectacle prescriptions help to rectify and limit any problems, particularly as operators become older.

The office where the secretary works is part of a local office complex close to where she lives. The company decentralised its office operations some years before, leaving only headquarters staff in offices in the centre of a big city.

The building where she works has been specially constructed to provide electronic office systems and is shared with similar 'satellite' offices belonging to other large companies. Close to the building there are also schools, health centres and other community services. This is important to her because it helps her in bringing up two children on her own.

Housekeeping the computer files

When she arrives at her workstation, she naturally looks in her electronic mailbox, where she finds a message from her boss reminding her that he wants the monthly sales report completed by 5 pm. She sighs and thinks, 'So much to do, so little time to do it.' Today she also has to start training a new word processing operator, attend a co-ordination meeting for other managers of executive support groups and comment on the latest design for a proposed new database system.

Firstly, however, she has to do some *housekeeping* on the departmental computer files in her role as local *data administrator*. A new sales executive has joined today. The secretary must allocate him file space in the database and a password. This she enters in the *data dictionary*, an important element within database management software which co-ordinates the use of the database.

She deletes the files and password related to the sales executive being replaced by the new man. She also 'tidies' up the departmental database, deleting files which members of the department have indicated are no longer needed.

Unless this housekeeping is done regularly, the database becomes unwieldy and takes up a lot of unnecessary disk space. *Hard disks*, made of a firm material like ordinary music records, are often used to store large volumes of database information. A floppy can typically hold a few hundred thousand characters, equivalent to a couple of hundred A4 pages. Hard disks can store millions of characters, equivalent to thousands of pages of text.

Burning up the word processor

The secretary has an hour or so before the new word processing operator comes from her initial interviews in the personnel department. So she decides to 'burn up' the word processor in a burst of high speed typing on the month's sales report.

In the old days, this report took a few days to get ready. It has a lot of columns summarising different sales figures, making typing fiddly and time consuming. The manager is also a bit obsessive about getting the phrasing of the text just right, and is liable to make lots of changes. There are usually a few sales figures coming in at the last minute which mean that chunks of the report have to be revised, leading to three of four draft revisions.

Now the secretary can do her high speed bash to get the first draft without having to worry about the layout. Her workstation's word processing software provides *columnar working* to shift columns to left or right, add or delete them automatically.

When operating as a word processor, her workstation's screen has a *tab rack* displayed on the top. This is equivalent to the ordinary tab settings that can be made on a manual typewriter. It can be set to establish margins and indentations. A *centring* feature ensures that headings are placed by the software in the centre between the margins.

The word processing software will put hyphens in the correct place when a word is cut off at the end of a line (*hyphenation*). A *wrapround* feature enables text to be typed without worrying about reaching the end of a line. The software automatically starts text on the next line as needed.

In tabular numerical working, of which there is a lot in the sales report, decimal points are automatically lined up. The software even helps eliminate *widows* – where there is a single line left on a new page or a single word on a line.

The secretary's workstation displays text in *proportional spacing*, in which characters have different widths, with 'i' the narrowest and 'm' the widest. She can therefore see exactly how the text will look when printed. The report is set with *right justification*. Text is straight at the right hand margin, with the software placing spaces to fill out the lines as necessary.

All these (and other) aids to final formatting allow the secretary to reach her maximum typing speed, which is much faster than it used to be on an electric typewriter.

Being taught by Mr Chips

Before the secretary has completed the first draft, the trainee word processing operator is brought down. The secretary files the report-so-far in computer memory and turns her attention to the newcomer.

The operator is being redeployed. She had been working in a clerical job that is being replaced by a new computer service. As part of the company's technology agreement, such reductions of employment in one part of the company are met by 'natural wastage' (not replacing people who leave voluntarily) and by retraining and redeploying staff to other parts of the company where staff are needed.

Trainee word processing operators get a full week's training plus regular supervision by the manager of executive support (our secretary) and monthly half-day revision training sessions in the first three months to discuss any on-the-job problems.

The word processing operator has already been on a two-day introduction course which covered electronic facilities in general. Today she is to start training on the systems she will be using.

Although the secretary is in charge of this phase of the training, she has relatively little to do, other than chatting to the operator, introducing her to other staff, and generally making her feel at ease. Her tutor will be Mr Chips – the word processor itself.

One of the reasons for selecting this word processor is that it is very *user friendly*: in other words, it treats the operator like a friend and makes its operation as easy as possible. It has its own

Computer Assisted Learning (CAL) software that instructs the newcomer how to use it.

CAL software provides the student with the relevant information. It then asks questions to test her grasp of the information. If she responds correctly, it will go to the next lesson. If she is wrong, it will patiently give more information before testing her again.

Once the operator has been through the CAL course on her own word processor, at her own pace, sitting in her new office surroundings, the secretary can be reasonably sure that the operator understands the basics of what to do. The CAL software also provides the secretary with a summary of the operator's learning performance which indicates any 'weak spots' where she took a long time. The secretary therefore knows what to focus attention on in follow-up discussions. Mr Chips does not disappear after the first tutorial. There is a HELP key on the word processor. If the operator is ever in doubt as to what to do, she presses HELP. The software will then advise her how to take the next step.

Daisies and dots the hard way

After setting the word processing operator off on her CAL course, the secretary returns to her workstation to finish off the first draft of the sales report. When it is done, she gets a printed version (*hard copy*) of the report that until now has existed only as digits in computer storage.

The department has two types of printer to produce hard copy. *Correspondence quality* (also called *letter quality*) material that needs to look good and be easy to read is produced on a *daisy wheel* printer. Otherwise, a *dot matrix* machine churns out the words.

A daisy wheel has a revolving typewheel with the characters held at the end of petal-like spokes (it is sometimes called a *petal* printer). The daisy wheel can be changed easily to provide a wide range of different type faces and characters.

This kind of *single element* print mechanism first became popular in the 1960s with the *golfball* electric typewriter. Instead of having a *typebasket* of separate print hammers, as in a manual typewriter, the raised characters are clustered around the single element, which moves until the character is over the point on the paper where it needs to be printed.

The daisy wheel produces high quality printed documents but is relatively slow, with speeds of around 20 to 50 characters a second. This means it can take a minute or more to print an A4 page. It can also be quite noisy.

A matrix printer creates characters on paper as a collection of dots formed when print needles hit the paper. These needles often come grouped in 5×7 or 9×14 clusters, but can be of much greater density. The more needle dots, the better the quality of the printed characters.

Generally, however, matrix printers are of a significantly lower quality, but quicker and quieter, than daisywheels. Dot matrix speeds go up to 400 characters per second or more, although correspondence-quality matrix printers tend to come down to daisy wheel speeds.

The secretary uses the matrix printer to get a hard copy of the first draft of the sales report. As the prime purpose of having a hard copy of the draft is that it should be marked up with corrections, it does not need to look pretty.

Group helping hands for executives

When it is ready, the secretary takes the copy of the first draft to the sales manager. Then she goes off to this month's meeting with the other managers of the executive support groups.

When word processors were first widely used in the 1970s, some companies moved many typists into word processing pools and reduced the number of secretaries, typists and clerks working for one manager. It was found that this often led to managers spending a lot of time doing their own clerical work, while typists found that working in a typing pool was monotonous because they no longer had personal contact with the people for whom they were typing.

Executive support groups (sometimes called *administrative support centres*) were set up to make efficient use of staff without reducing the benefits that come from having close personal liaison between managers and their secretarial and clerical staff. Each group contains a mix of staff offering a variety of electronic office services to a number of managers and professionals.

Staff in support groups have the scope for career development and the opportunity to do a variety of work. Our secretary, for example, is a local data administrator, a representative on the technical systems design team, and has other supervisory and managerial responsibilities.

She has a considerable degree of control in working with her staff to decide how they want to organise the allocation of duties, provided they give a satisfactory overall service. This aids personal job satisfaction for the staff and allows problems to be sorted out within and between groups by those who understand the real working demands.

Down in the response time dumps

The secretary and other support group managers get together for a working salad-lunch in the executive meeting room. They find the informal exchanges of work experiences as important as the main business of the meeting, so they like a relaxed atmosphere. The meeting covers a wide range of topics, from current problems to long-term strategies.

Two of the most important immediate issues at their meeting relate to *response times* and *dumps*. A response time is how long the system takes to provide a reply to a request that has been keyed in. A dump is when the system transfers information from one part of storage to another in case of a system breakdown.

The meeting considers results of tests to monitor response times in two areas of activities where staff have made a lot of complaints. In one case, staff receive enquiries over the telephone and then use a VDU to get an answer. Their complaint has been that the response time has been getting too slow, which puts them under pressure from the person making the enquiry.

A deterioration in response time often happens when more terminals are added to a computer-based information service. The increased demand puts strains on the controlling software and the hardware at its command to respond to each terminal. The support groups have gathered enough information to show the deterioration has been significant in the last month. They agree to ask for an increase in computer processing and memory capability to overcome the problem.

Ironically, the other response time problem is that the system can be too quick in some cases. A number of staff spend a lot of their time interacting with the computer. They feel that the system puts pressure on them by responding too quickly when asking them for the next piece of information. Tests found the response time for these users was within the standard limit (two seconds is regarded as a reasonable response time in most cases).

The meeting agreed to recommend an experiment where the system is 'slugged' to respond a bit slower. The experiment will be assessed by *human factors* consultants who specialise in understanding the psychological and behavoural aspects of using new technology.

The dumping problem mainly affected word processing operators. There is nothing more infuriating in word processing than to find, halfway through typing a long report that the computer loses the stored information. The system is therefore programmed to dump to backing store at regular intervals so that, if something goes wrong, the operator can *restore* the files to their state when last dumped, rather than having to start all over again.

There have been a few complaints that the dumping system had failed. The meeting felt it could not decide yet whether these were caused by operators misusing the system or a computer problem. It is decided to keep monitoring the situation.

Principal misuses of word processing

Another issue discussed by the support managers is the training of *principals*. This is the term used for those executives, professionals and others who originate material for the word processor. Although the company provides them with training in word processing, support staff still feel principals are being wasteful and loading unnecessary word processing work onto them.

When word processing first came in, one of the main secretarial complaints was that too many principals still loved 'cut-and-paste' methods of revising a draft. They would chop up a hard copy draft if text was to be moved and stick it together in the right order. This is totally unsuitable for word processing.

The company subsequently started training courses on word processing for principals, which overcame such rudimentary problems. The main accusation of misuse discussed by the meeting is that principals lack discipline in the way they use word processing capabilities. Altering and moving around text on a word processor is so easy that principals continue to make changes long after the text should have been finalised.

This wastes the time of the word processing operators and leads to an excessive amount of paper being used for hard copy. In cases where the principals do their own word processing, such constant revision does not matter as it is all done on the screen relatively quickly. Where there is a constant to-ing and fro-ing of drafts, however, it is inefficient and annoying.

The meeting heard that the training department has agreed to add an extra half day to principals' training at which a representative of the support groups would discuss such problems. The training department itself will include more material discussing why the principals should be more careful with word processing.

Juggling with text

The other main topic at the support manager's meeting is a new database system. Agreement is reached on the main points to be raised by the secretary when she represents them later in the day at a systems design meeting. The support managers finish their discussions in time for the secretary to get back to her workstation to finish off the sales report.

After getting the corrected draft from the sales manager, she returns to her workstation. The sales manager has marked the draft in the right way, clearly indicating the points at which text needs to be changed.

The secretary goes through the draft and calls up the appropriate text on the screen. The cursor, a square blob, points to the place in the text where she is working. If she is to delete a word, say, she moves the cursor to the start of the word and presses a key marked DELETE WORD. She goes through the report adding a word here, deleting a character there, eliminating a sentence, shifting a paragraph.

The screen is the secretary's window onto the text held in computer storage. She can 'navigate' her way through the text by moving (*scrolling*) the screen window up and down (*vertical* scrolling) and right and left (*horizontal* scrolling) until the text to be edited is on the display. The secretary is pleased that her workstation has *smooth* scrolling. On some other systems, the text moves jerkily during scrolling, which can be a strain on the eyes.

Some late news which the manager received via electronic mail confirmed the name of a new product that is frequently referred to in the report by its development codename. Instead of having to find each place in the report where the code name is used and replace it with the new name, the secretary instructs the word processor to do a *global exchange*. This *search and replace* method automatically looks for every occurrence of the text to be changed and replaces it with the correct text. When she has completed all this editing, the secretary transfers the report to the electronic 'In tray' of the sales manager. He will do the final editing. When he is happy with the report, he gets it printed on a daisy wheel printer and also sends electronic mail copies immediately to the chief executive and finance director of the company.

Users in the driving seat

Meanwhile, the secretary spends a little time with the new word processing operator before going to the meeting to discuss the design of the new database system. When the secretary had first joined the company, it was unknown for secretarial staff to become involved in the design and selection of new systems.

In the past, technical specialists – called *systems analysts* – would investigate the requirements of the system, talking to managers and a few staff to find out how things worked – and how they might with the new system. This often led to computer-based systems which worked technically but failed to meet real working needs because the analyst had developed an idealised formal picture of how things *should* function, not how they actually do.

This company now insists that users of any new system, at all levels, should participate directly in the design, evaluation, development and implementation of any electronic office project. This has generally resulted in systems which are more effective because they are closer to what users want.

The secretary is on the file management project as a representative of all executive support groups. Her own knowledge gained as a local data administrator has meant that she has also joined a working party on data administration. Her main responsiblity on the systems design team, however, is to ensure that the software is acceptable to the support staff who will use it.

She has therefore received training in human factors (also known as *ergonomic*) techniques which study the way people interact with technology and which aim to achieve maximum effectiveness by trying to make users comfortable with the technology and more satisfied with their jobs.

Making the computer friendly

Many computer-based systems have been extremely unfriendly to the user. The dialogue between the user and the system has often involved complicated operating rules and jargon-ruined language, frequently incomprehensible to the non-computer specialists.

Involvement of users in the design is one way in which this unfriendliness has been overcome, coupled with the application of human factors techniques. For any file management or database system, a key human factors consideration to resolve is the kinds of *query language* and *information retrieval* techniques used to search through the computerised information store.

The menu method, described in the telebanking example early in this chapter, is an information retrieval technique particularly suited to a newcomer to the system. It 'hand-holds' the user in a step-by-step movement to find what is wanted. For an experienced user, however, menu systems can become a laborious nuisance.

Another relatively easy retrieval method for some databases is *Query-By-Example (QBE)*. With this, the user keys in an example of the item(s) being searched for, say, a company name and a town if a list of all branches of a particular store in a town is needed. The example name and town must be placed in the spaces on the screen that indicate a company name and town are expected.

Instruction and response is a method where the computer asks questions to which the user replies. *Keyword* searching is done by having the user specify the key characteristics being looked for, such as 'FIND all employees over 35 and who speak French or who have over 10 years sales experience'. *Full text search*, which is often used with word processing work, allows the user to look for a whole chunk of text.

There are many more query techniques, each with its particular advantages and disadvantages, depending on the nature of the database, the type of task being done and the expertise of the user. To get back to our secretary – the support managers have delegated the secretary to push for two main requirements.

Firstly, the design team should give users the option to choose the type of query method. Newcomers, for example, should be given a menu *interface* but, as they gain experience, they should be allowed to switch to say, a keyboard search.

Secondly, before deciding which user interfaces to use, *pilot experiments* should be set up where users have a chance of trying out different techniques without being under usual business pressures. These experiments should be evaluated by a human factors consultant.

Two of the technical experts on the team argue that providing optional interfaces would add too much to the overall cost of the system and that pilot experiments would delay the system. The general agreement, however, is that these matters are so crucial that they should be accepted. The technicians are asked to quantify the extra costs of having more than one method and the secretary is asked to draw up a tight schedule for pilot experiments.

It is the end of a busy day. When the database meeting is over, the secretary returns to her room for her coat. She is satisfyingly tired and smiles to herself on the short bus ride home. Tonight it is the turn of her teenage son to make dinner.

Starting the day with an electronic tickler

The final glimpse at an electronic office day is through the eyes of a middle manager, the assistant manager in the housing department of a local government authority. We will linger on him less than the managing director and secretary because their days have already brought in many of the electronic office systems used by the assistant manager.

His day also begins by opening his electronic mailbox. After dealing with urgent messages, he is tickled. The authority's system includes a *tickler file* facility. This automatically reminds him of important meetings and other actions he should take.

Today, the tickler reminds him that he has to attend an important meeting in two days, by which time he must complete work he was asked to do at the previous meeting. As if this reminder is not enough, the tickler has brought forward the minutes of the last meeting into his electronic 'In tray' where all the items refering to him are highlighted in *reverse video*, with particularly urgent matters *blinking*.

The assistant manager had set up this brought-forward tickler file soon after the previous meeting and had specified which matter should be in reverse video and blinking. Normally his workstation displays orange characters on a brown background. Parts of the text in reverse video are shown as brown characters on an orange background. Blinking makes certain characters or words flash on and off.

The assistant manager has carried out most of the actions. The most important unfinished task is to check on the current results from the *expert systems* project. Expert systems can 'reason' and advise in the same way as an experienced human expert.

Tools of the information trade

The assistant manager is in charge of a project to develop an expert system to assist people to find their way through the regulations which govern the payment of housing welfare benefits. In order to carry out this responsibility, he has had to learn how to use various software development aids. He has done this mainly through the Authority's *information centre.*

In the past, all the computing specialists in the Authority worked for the *Data Processing (DP)* department, which originally grew up around the large central *(mainframe)* computer. As the micro lead to the spread of *Distributed Data Processing (DDP)* that placed computing capabilities closer to where people worked, the DP Department found it difficult to cope with the increased demand from users.

The Authority therefore set up a number of information centres to give advice, training and hands-on access to the range of computing services available. These centres have a mix of stand-alone systems and terminals with many software packages – the tools of the information trade.

His local centre has trained him in software development techniques for expert systems. He can also walk into the centre to use various systems that are not available from his workstation, which is primarily designed for electronic mail activities. Although he has computing specialists on the project, his training has helped him to keep the project on the right track and allows him to question the technical specialists without being bamboozled by their replies.

Voices in the electronic wastebin

The assistant manager fires off electronic memos to everyone in the project to report on their work. Then he returns to some routine work he had been doing the night before. He presses a key marked DESKTOP on his workstation. This brings back the documents he was working on last night.

He spends about an hour at the workstation preparing a report, answering and writing memos. His *executive workstation* has many features to simplify his use of electronic office facilities.

For example, there is a telephone handset and loudspeaker built into the workstation and also some keys that are similar to those on a tape recorder (forward, rewind, stop, etc). He can use this to dictate memos which he then sends electronically to his executive support centre for word processing. He can also use it for *voicegrams* (or *voice memos*).

When he speaks into the handset his voice is recorded – not on magnetic tape but as digits in computer memory, in exactly the same way as text produced from a word processor. Voices can therefore be interspersed with text.

The assistant manager sent a memo to his boss the previous day. He has now received it back in the electronic mail. The returned memo has a couple of ikons which indicate that it has been *annotated* with a voice gram. The assistant manager positions the cursor over an ikon, pushes a key and, as if by magic, his boss' voice comes booming out on the loudspeaker.

Having checked all the voicegrams, the assistant manager then presses the WASTEBIN key. This tells the system that the memo is to be destroyed, but not immediately. At the end of the day, a housekeeping software routine automatically 'empties' (deletes) information in the wastebin files. During the day, information can be rescued from the electronic wastebin, just as you can fish a piece of paper out of a real bin. The electronic information, however, will not be crumpled and tea stained.

Hunting-the-bugs conferences

The assistant manager then goes off to a meeting to discuss errors (*bugs*) in the software. Legend has it that a recurring problem at an early pioneering computer installation was cured when someone opened the processor's cabinet, and out flew a moth. 'Bugs' have been plaguing computers ever since.

Today he is holding an *audio-conference*. Project staff gather in sound-proof rooms close to their offices. They can talk to each other via telephone communications. They do not need hand-pieces to talk and listen. Microphones and loudspeakers in the room allow them to sit around a table and talk, as if everyone is in the same room.

Each meeting room also has a facsimile device so that documents can be exchanged quickly. There are also workstations in each room to aid communications.

The Authority is also experimenting with *video-conferencing*. This adds pictures to voice and fax. Cameras in the meeting room transmit video pictures to other rooms. This costs more than audio-conferencing and many people feel awkward with it, so the Authority is not using it yet as widely as audio-conferencing.

Bugs can be difficult to track down. As a back-up to other meetings, the assistant manager makes extensive use of *computer-conferencing* facilities. He has established a 'bug file' in the departmental information network that can be read from and written to by anyone on the project. This allows a continuing discussion to take place between people separated geographically and not available always at the same time.

For example, he recently put into the bug file the symptoms of a particularly tricky problem and his thoughts on what the cause may be. Over the previous week, others in the project had added their own views and other evidence of the problem. At the audio-conferencing meeting, the informal computer-conferencing dialogue was scanned to provide invaluable assistance in eradicating this resilient bug.

Slimming the middle manager spread

At lunch time, the assistant manager meets an ex-colleague who recently opted for early retirement. There has been a noticeable slimming of the ranks of middle managers and administrators since electronic office systems were widely introduced by the Authority.

'After all, our main job was to push paper between the top men and the people who did the work,' muses his ex-colleague over a glass of wine. 'When the amount of paper work dropped, our days were numbered.'

Middle management had been one of the major growth areas in office work. Many organisations became portly, with a spare tyre of middle managers who did not have the power to make major decisions and were also not in direct charge of day-to-day operations.

New office technology enables top management to communicate more quickly and directly with operational levels. Instead of calling on middle managers to feed them information, top executives can get the information they want (and more) by moving no further than their workstation.

Many of the decisions which middle managers make can be automated. 'I don't have much discretion left in deciding whether to give a mortgage loan under our First Time Buyer scheme,' sighs the assistant manager. 'People just go to a council office, sit at a VDU and answer questions. Then I get a list of the computer's recommendations. I could over-rule the computer but I'm not going to stick my neck out.'

'I suppose middle managers have been pretty good filters, sifting out some of the rubbish which emanates from the top,' remarks his ex-colleague cynically. 'Oh yes, you are right,' replies the assistant manager. 'We have had a few dust-ups recently because the chief executive has broadcast new edicts to everyone through electronic mail before we have had a chance to tone them down for local consumption.'

They then slip into some 'good old days' reminiscences before the assistant manager returns to his office, pensively contemplating his future.

Electronic doesn't mean paperless

For most of the afternoon, the assistant manager does not use any electronic office systems. He concentrates on reading through a file from tenants on a housing estate which has been experiencing problems with maintenance and repairs. This file is in a manilla cardboard folder, in an old fashioned steel filing cabinet, and all the information is on paper.

Although a lot of information is handled in electronic form, a great deal of paper is still used in the office. The department's printers are in almost constant use producing external correspondence and some internal documents and drafts that need to be in hard copy form.

Technological enthusiasts sometimes forget what a handy and useful medium paper can be as a way of holding and communicating information. It is still the best method in many circumstances. Even if it were desirable to have everything in electronic form, there are still technical problems about getting information into computer code.

If information is originated on a workstation, there is no

problem about keeping it in electronic form. Much of the correspondence received by the Authority, however, is in hand-written or other form that is not easy to get transferred to computer digital codes. The Authority does have some *Optical Character Recognition (OCR)* devices which can recognise typed characters automatically and put them into electronic code.

The OCR readers are used for tasks where information is typed in a standard form on a lot of documents. They are too slow, unreliable and expensive to be used on, say, typewritten letters which contain corrections and crooked lines.

Information going outside can be sent by electronic mail only if the recipients can receive electronic mail. Universal electronic mail, equivalent to the easy exchange of information between telephone users, is still not possible, although the Authority has instituted some information services available to homes via a local cable network, which also provides other multi-channel TV and information services.

1984 and all that Big Brother talk

Later on, the assistant manager attends a meeting with elected councillors to discuss the protection of private information held within the computerised information system. Some people see computer-based systems as the embodiment of Orwell's all pervasive Big Brother in his novel *Nineteen Eighty-Four*.

The reason for collecting information in a database is that it can be made accessible quickly and flexibly to many people, in many places, through networks of workstations. This could be a powerful weapon in the hands of an organisation or individual wishing to keep people under surveillance or to use facts to a person's disadvantage.

Many countries have therefore passed *data protection* legislation to try to protect people from such invasions of privacy. Data protection laws give people the right, for example, to check the accuracy of information about themselves and to insist that information collected for one purpose (say, housing or medical records) is not used for another purpose (such as checking on a person's credit worthiness or suitability as an applicant for a job). See Chapter 7 for further details on data protection.

The Authority has taken considerable care to meet its legal obligations and has produced its own set of guidelines The electronic information system has many inbuilt checks, such as the need to give passwords before certain files can be read. Some sensitive information is transmitted in *encrypted* form, as a spy message might be, so that even if someone taps the line, it will be very difficult to crack the secret code.

The assistant manager discusses with the councillors some examples where citizens feel the computer information has been misused. Most of these were caused by operator errors or by staff over-reaching their powers, for which they have been reprimanded.

There is one worrying case which could indicate a flaw in the security procedures. The assistant manager takes responsibility for investigating it and reporting back to the councillors within a week.

Before leaving for the day, he sets his tickler file to keep him reminded of this problem. He files away his electronic 'desktop' and turns out the office lights. Silently and unseen, the electronic housekeeper comes alive, busily emptying the electronic wastebins.

Now is the hour

This chapter is not science fiction. Every example of new office technology is available now. There are organisations already using the systems described. There are people who work, at least partly, in the new patterns encapsulated in the examples.

In this chapter you have seen examples of the four main aspects of any electronic office:

1 *Document production*: word processing and printers.
2 *Filing and information retrieval*: databases and file management systems, query methods.
3 *Communications*: electronic mail.
4 *Decision support*: spreadsheets, modelling, access to information.

These basic elements are the source of a cascade of imaginative possibilities.

You have also seen a glimpse of some of the changes in working lifestyles (some home-based work, more local office centres) and in the type of work done. The fictionalised environments have been painted with an optimistic brush, illustrating 'best practice' methods of organising electronic office work. It won't always be so pleasant.

Technological and social sparks will fly in the electronic office, illuminating and enriching some lives but hurting and diminishing others, unless care is taken to protect those who might be victims rather than victors. Chapters 4 and 5 provide advice on how to accentuate the positive and eliminate the negative in the electronic office.

The next chapter, however, is a very brief summary of some important technological ideas and jargon. It provides further help in understanding what advertisements, sales brochures, manuals, techno-whizzes and others are trying to tell you.

3 Ins and outs of electronic boxes

More about the technology

So far, this book has described what new office technology does.
Along the way, aspects of the technology have been mentioned
and some necessary jargon has been infiltrated. Before moving
on to examine how people and organisations can best harness
its tremendous power, this chapter pauses for a more lingering
look at computer-based technology.

It recaps on some of the techniques and equipment already
mentioned and discusses devices and methods not yet touched
on. Chapter 8 can be read later if you want to know more about
the history of information technology and the industries spawned
by these innovations.

How a word processor works

There are four main elements in word processing:

1 *Input*: getting information in.
2 *Memory/storage*: remembering what has been input.
3 *Processing*: doing something with the information under software control.
4 *Output*: getting information out again.

In addition, most systems should have a *communications* capability
to link them to other systems.

Figure 2 illustrates how these are put together in a stand alone
word processor. When you sit at a word processor, the most
obvious pieces of hardware are the keyboard (input) and screen
(output). There is also usually a disk drive and some floppy disks
around to store programs and information; disks can also be
used for input and output. A printer is used for hard copy output.

Out of sight, inside the keyboard or in a separate box, are
silicon micro chips. Some of these are microprocessors used for
what is called the *Central Processing Unit (CPU)*. Others are for
main memory to hold information needed immediately by the

processor. *Read Only Memory (ROM)* contains software that is permanently needed; these chips cannot have the information in them overwritten. *Random Access Memory (RAM)* would be better known as Write and Read Memory because information in it can be written to, as well as read from.

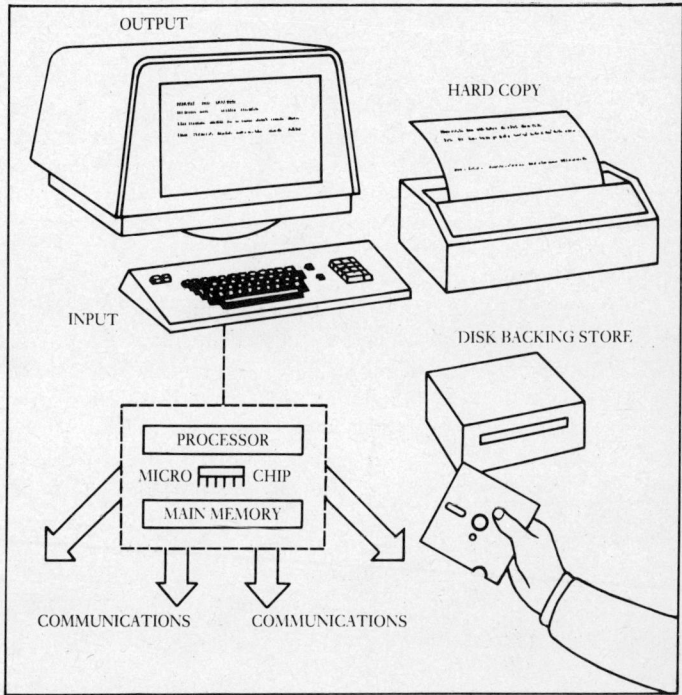

Figure 2: Basic elements of a word processor. Keyboard, screen, disks and drive are visible. Chip memory and processors are in the keyboard or another container.

Microprocessors can operate at hundreds of thousands, even millions of actions per second, so main memory has to be something that can also act quickly, like silicon chips. Chips, however, are relatively expensive as a storage medium. RAM chips can also lose information when the power is switched off (this is called *volatile* memory.)

Floppy disks are therefore needed as a means of keeping permanently stored software and information files. These can be used to load software into the system, or to store the draft of a report once it has been keyed in, then to input that draft for editing.

The keyboard should be separate from the screen and it should be possible to rotate and tilt the screen (see Chapters 5 and 7 for more on the design of screens and keyboards). In a *shared resource* (or *shared logic*) system, word processor workstations share common processors, main memory, backing storage and printers.

A chip is a tiny piece of silicon. For operational purposes, this is mounted on a plastic strip with wire 'legs' to make electrical connections. What you may see when you look at a microprocessor or memory chip is a strange, spidery object, as depicted in Figure 2.

Ditto for microcomputers, etc

Any computer-based system, from a home microcomputer through the variety of systems discussed in Chapter 1 to the largest supercomputer, has the same basic elements as a word processor. The form of the *Input/Output (I/O)*, storage and even processor can vary enormously, as discussed later in the chapter and in Chapter 8. Beneath the shell, however, they are all *data* blood brothers (data is a computerish word meaning 'information').

A typical business microcomputer is also likely to have a screen, keyboard, chip main memory and CPU, and similar *peripherals* to a word processor, such as floppy disks and printers. 'Peripheral' is a general name given to I/O and backing store devices.

Data files for business uses are generally much larger than word processor files, so a business micro is likely to have hard disks. A popular form of hard disk with micros is the *cartridge disk* which has the disk in a sealed cartridge that can be as small as 5 inches or less in diameter but contains millions of characters of information. It is also known as a *Winchester* disk, the codename used by IBM when developing the prototype.

Larger computers have *disk packs*, which consist of a number of hard disks on a spindle, contained in a sealed plastic pack. These can be loaded onto a disk drive when needed. Magnetic tape is also widely used for storage, either in the form of *reel-to-reel* tapes on large systems or cassette tapes for home micros. Tapes are much slower, less capacious and have more restrictive information handling capabilities than disks.

Bits, nibbles, bytes and the special K

'Bits' and 'bytes' are terms you are likely to bump into as soon as you come near any computer-based system. *Bit* is an abbreviation for *bi*nary dig*it*. Eight bits are called a *byte*. A *byte* is usually the unit used to encode a character. (A *nibble* is half a byte, 4 bits.)

The size of computer main memory and backing store media is usually given in terms of bytes; you can regard this as being equivalent to the number of characters that can be stored. Sizes are also often given with the letter 'K' or 'M', such as '16K bytes' or '5M bytes'. You can take K to mean one thousand and M to equal one million.

In computing, however, K actually equals 1024 (2^{10}) and M is 1 048 576 (2^{20}). In binary arithmetic, multiples of 2 are as significant as multiples of 10 in ordinary decimal arithmetic (1000, for example, is 10^3). You therefore often find numbers in computing that are multiples of 2, such as 8, 16, 32, and so on.

Bits are also often mentioned in relation to the size of a processor. You may hear about an '8-bit' or 16-bit' machine. This does *not* mean it has only 8 or 16 bits of memory but it does indicate the power of the processor used.

Each processor is regarded as being divided into *words* containing a fixed number of bits. These words are used as the basic building block for handling data and for the *instruction set*, which are the basic machine actions that can be manipulated by software.

The size of this word length governs the range and variety that can be offered by the instruction set and also the amount of main memory that can be handled efficiently. All you really need to remember about this is that, generally, the longer the bit length of a system, the more potential power and capability it has.

The degree to which such increased potentiality is realised depends to a great extent on having software available that exploits the full capability.

Software: from underware to firmware

The software that helps you to edit text on a word processor or to handle a company's accounts is known as *applications software*. Such programs directly carry out the tasks requested by the user. There are many layers of software beneath this level, a kind of 'underware' beneath the outer software clothing.

The first digital computers could be programmed only in the basic instruction set of the system, the *machine code*. Unbelievable as it may seem today, the instructions of the programs were written laboriously in their binary (0/1) code.

As programs grew more complex, it became obvious that programming had to be made easier. The first step was to create *low level* (also called *assembly*) languages. These have the same format as machine code but use mnemonic codes to make the instructions easier to remember and write down. For example, ADS could mean 'ADed into Store'. Numbers in an assembly language can be expressed in decimal form.

Low level languages make efficient use of the machines resources but are still relatively difficult to learn and time consuming to use. *High level languages* have therefore been developed that use English words (mainly because of the American dominance of computing developments) and match the kinds of application tasks being carried out. For example, Cobol is the most popular high level language for commercial tasks, Fortran for scientific uses, and Basic on micros and for people learning programming.

High level languages need a degree of programming skill that most users do not have the time or inclination to gain. *Program generators, applications* and *end-user* languages enable users to create programs without being aware that they are doing so. They allow users to follow their 'natural' way of carrying out a task, eliciting information from the user to generate the required code automatically.

Some applications programs allow the user to tailor the system to their special requirements. A number of factors, called *variables* or *parameters,* are not finalised in the software until the user gives them appropriate values. This is sometimes known as parameter-driven software.

Processors can run programs only in binary language. Software 'underware' is therefore needed to translate programming languages into machine code. *Compilers* translate high level languages; *interpreters* are compilers that translate high level statements one at a time rather than having to have the whole program before it gets to work. *Assemblers* translate low level languages (which are sometimes called assemblers, as well as assembly languages).

A compiler is an example of *systems software*, which deals with how the system operates rather than controlling applications directly. An *operating system* is a collection of systems software routines that co-ordinate the hardware resources and the workload running on it. Applications software is often written to run under an operating system rather than for a particular type of hardware. CP/M, MS–DOS and Unix are examples of popular operating systems on microcomputers.

Software is usually held on backing store, then input (*loaded*) into main memory. Some systems software, such as compilers, are often provided on ROM so are permanently in main memory. Software fixed into chip circuitry like this is called *firmware*.

A computing Tower of Babel

Computer-based systems do not always get on with each other. Each processor has its own machine code and assembler, which is not recognised by machines with other processors.

Although high level languages were originally aimed at encouraging the creation of software that could be easily moved from one machine to another, languages tended to develop their own dialects. These dialects are instilled into compilers, which then cannot understand programs in other dialects of the same language. Some languages, like Cobol, have been good at ironing out dialects to create genuinely *portable* software. Others, like Basic, have remained a Tower of Babel.

As if these software incompatibilities were not enough, computers also 'talk' different languages when they record information. If you take a floppy disk with output from one word processor and try to use it as input to another make of word processor, you will probably find that it will be incomprehensible to the second machine. The actual format of the disks, as well as the information on it, can cause incompatibilities.

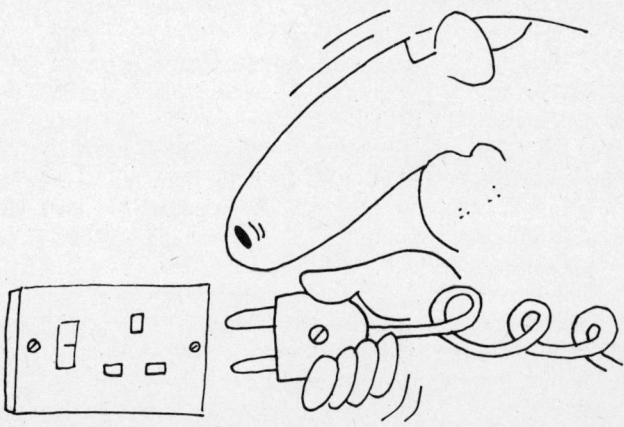

You may wish to use word processor output as a direct input to a phototypesetter, a computer-controlled machine for producing properly printed output. Once again, you may find that the machines do not talk to each other.

The problem is that output is encoded in a unique way by each system. The code, for example, indicating 'start a new line' on one word processor could be different to the code used on another machine for the same action. To move disks from one machine to another, you either need special conversion software that translates from one code to another or the alterations have to be made laboriously via the keyboard of the originating system.

Barriers to communication

Compatibility problems are compounded when computer-based devices have to communicate with each other.

Before they actually transmit information, two devices must have a handshaking 'chat' to establish contact. They have to do the equivalent of saying, 'Hi, are you there?' 'Yes I am here.' 'Are you ready to receive?' 'Ready. Roger and out.'

Very strict *protocols* have to be followed in these exchanges. And, sure enough, protocols are different on systems from different manufacturers, or even on various types of device from the same manufacturer.

Protocol converters and *communications interfaces* have been developed to overcome these problems. One of the main advantages of local area networks, discussed in Chapter 1, is that they make it easier to link various workstations and computers.

These practical difficulties are a major hindrance to the growth of electronic offices and other information technology applications. National and international bodies have devoted a lot of energy to developing standards in software, information storage and communications – and trying to get them to stick.

The 'super-telex' teletex is an example of a service with clearly defined common rules. The International Standards Organisation (ISO) has also established a layered framework for *open systems* communications, which should lead to computer devices being connected with the ease that telephone subscribers are hooked up to each other.

Nevertheless, you should always be alert to possible compatibility problems. Internationally agreed standards take time to implement and are frequently obeyed loosely and patchily. Commercial manufacturers often make claims about compatibility which, when investigated, turn out to have crucial exceptions that invalidate the claims.

You could find, for example, that a program which runs under the control of one brand-name operating system on one micro-computer, fails to run on an operating system with the same name on another machine. Operating systems can vary in how they are implemented.

I/O, I/O, its off to work we go

The most common form of input to a computer now comes from a keyboard. At one time it was with *punched cards* and *punched paper tape*. In the future it might be by voice and handwriting.

On a punched card or paper tape, the absence of presence of holes indicate the 'o' or 'I' value for a binary digit. A boom area of clerical work in the 1960s was *data preparation (data prep)*, where operators transferred information from written or typed documents onto punched cards using keyboards to prepare the cards.

Data prep began to fade when more VDUs came into use for *direct data entry*. Instead of first being written down and then sent to data prep for putting onto cards, information began to be keyed in directly from the VDUs.

In offices, a keyboard is the obvious medium for use in typing jobs, like word processing. A keyboard is an easy form of input for computers to understand. When you press the 'A' key, there is no doubt about your intention. The pressure on the key triggers a signal that sends the computer code for 'A' into computer storage.

Just think, however, how each person's handwriting is unique and how people have an infinite number of ways of pronouncing letters and words when they speak. You can clearly see the difficulties of getting computers to understand handwriting and speech.

There are systems which can recognise handwriting and voices but only in relatively limited contexts. For example, there are *voice recognition* systems that can be trained to understand a particular person saying a certain number of words spoken in isolation, with pauses between each word. More advanced systems can understand *continuous speech*, which is the usual way of speaking, without pausing between words. Such systems can operate only in specific contexts and with special vocabularies.

Other input methods have been discussed earlier in the book, such as Optical Character Recognition to read printed words and light pens to 'draw' on the screens of graphics terminals. More sophisticated OCR equipment can read most printed text but is unable to read typed material that has crooked lines and handwritten insertions. Limitations in speech understanding, handwriting and some typed and printed input are major constraints on what information can be handled electronically.

Putting the word out

Output is relatively easy compared to input. The information is already in digital code. When it has to be presented to the outside world, the computer triggers output devices from its known base of information rather than having to interpret human input that may be difficult to understand.

Displays and printers ure the most popular output forms. A word processor, VDU or microcomputer screen is usually based on a *Cathode Ray Tube (CRT)*, just like an ordinary TV set.

Flat screens are also available, similar to those used in digital watches and calculators. *Liquid Crystal Displays (LCDs)* create characters by applying tiny voltages across a cell containing a liquid crystal substance, usually making dark characters on a lighter background. *Light Emitting Diodes (LEDs)* are made of a semiconductor, like gallium arsenide, that glows (usually red), when stimulated. LEDs need more power than LCDs; in watches, you often have to press a button to see what is on a LED display.

Daisy wheel and dot matrix are *impact printers* that make images on paper by a device that physically hits the paper. There are also *non-impact printers*. High speed *laser* printers, for example, create images using laser lights; *ink jet* printers squirt ink dots at the paper; *thermal* printers use heat sensitive paper; and *electrosensitive* devices print on electrically sensitive paper. Phototypesetters can be used to produce printed material from word processing output.

Voice output can be produced by digitally recording human voices saying words and phrases, then playing them back under software control. Artificial *synthesised* voices, as used in 'talking' cars, games and educational devices, can also be used for voice output.

Computer-controlled synthesised sounds can be used to imitate musical instruments and to sound remarkably like human voices. However, just because a system has human-like output should not lead you to think it is any more 'human' or 'intelligent' than systems with any other type of output.

In design, medical and scientific work, graph plotters can produce drawings, graphs, maps, and so on. *Computer Output to Microfilm (COM)* provides output onto strips of fine grain film or *microfiche*, a 'card' form of microfilm.

Memories are made of this

As has already been discussed, chips for main memory and magnetic media for backing store are the most popular ways of storing digital computer information. Bits are represented by circuits and electronic pulses on chips. Magnetic media store information according to the direction of magnetisation of tiny magnets in the surface.

With a magnetic disk you can go directly to the information you want (*direct* or *random access*), in the same way that you can go directly to the track you want on a music record. For information on tape, however, you have to search through the whole tape (*serial access*) before you find what you want, again just as with a music tape. This makes disks faster and more suitable for holding large amounts of information.

A relatively new and potentially important innovation in computer-linked storage is video. *Video tape*, the same as used in home video cassette records, can be linked to a Computer Assisted Learning program. A snatch of video is shown, the software asks questions about it, the student answers, and more video is shown or the same pieces reshown, depending on the answers. This is known as *interactive video*.

Video tape, like magnetic tape, is a serial storage method that has to be read through to find what you want. *Video disks*, which also can be bought with entertainment films recorded on them, provide a more flexible direct access way of storing still and moving pictures. Videos always use digital storage, even for entertainment shows.

Video disks are a more efficient and effective means of providing interactive video than video tape. Video disks also provide a method of *electronic filing*. A disk can hold images of 50,000 or more pages of text, pictures, diagrams, etc. Provided suitable information retrieval software is available, this can be used as a 'super' electronic filing cabinet. Information on video disk cannot, however, be edited or otherwise processed because it is stored as a kind of electronic photograph and so not all the text and diagrams are in digital code.

Magnetic and video media involve the use of mechanical methods to drive the storage. Chips are known as *solid state*, with no need for any moving parts. *Bubble memory* is a form of solid state large volume mass memory, particularly popular in portable terminals and microcomputers. With this, bits are stored on tiny magnetic 'bubbles' in a material, such as garnet.

Even the copier gets brainy

Various input, output and storage devices can be combined in kaleidoscopic ways to create useful devices. A good example of the versatility of computer-based information technology is the *intelligent copier*, sometimes called the *intelligent copier/printer*.

An ordinary copier makes a xerographic 'picture' of the original document. Fax transmission sends a copy of a document across a telecommunications link. With neither of these methods can you do anything to the information on the original, other than copy it.

If you add a processor, storage and additional I/O to a fax, lots of new opportunities open up. For example, with OCR equipment, you can automatically input to computer store the text in documents that are to be 'copied'. Diagrams and other images can be *digitised* for subsequent manipulation, or simply copied using fax techniques.

Text read into the intelligent copier by OCR can subsequently be edited from a word processor that can also insert new text. Multiple copies of documents can then be transmitted by fax using stored programs containing various distribution lists. Other programs can offer many other facilities.

It is yet another example of the many faces of software-hearted, micro-virile electronic office technology.

Now the spotlight moves to people

The first three chapters of the book have focused on the technology: what it is, how it works, how it operates in action, the new services it offers. If your technological thirst is still unslaked, there are some more drams in Chapter 8.

The spotlight now switches to centre stage. To the people who choose and use new office technology. To the organisations, big and small, who look to the electronic office to improve efficiency and to open up new opportunities. To the individuals and groups whose lives face great challenges as the electronic office spreads through society.

4 Taming the technology

The office evo-revolution

There is a joke about a stranger lost in the countryside. He meets a local lad walking his dog. 'What's the best way to the big city,' asks the stranger. 'If I were you, I wouldn't start from here,' is the answer.

The same thing is true with new office technology. The best route to the electronic office is to start from scratch and build a new office organisation around new technology. Most companies and organisations, however, cannot start from the ideal position. They must move on from where they find themselves.

Organisations start with existing office procedures; staff with experience of traditional office methods; organisational structures and working methods developed over many years; personnel policies and labour relations machinery honed through years of give and take between management and staff.

Many organisations already have some form of computing, from micros and stand-alone word processors to large systems run by data processing departments. Because of the incompatibilities between computers, it is not possible to scrap existing systems and start again with new ones the next day.

Existing computer systems have also often become ingrained in the way organisations operate. Any change to the computer can send shock-waves through the organisation. The most appealing route to the electronic office is by 'evo-revolution' – short term evolution, long term revolution. Eventually, there will be a revolution in office work. Progress towards it should be at an evolutionary, step-by-step pace.

Beware the rolling bandwagon

Some techno-enthusiasts like to believe that the best way to get to the electronic office is to hitch a lift on the nearest technological bandwagon, which will automatically deliver the goodies in due time. Many organisations and individuals can testify to the costly foolishness of this belief.

The first wave of commercial computing that began in the 1960s caused some casualties. Companies invested large sums of money in a technology which often failed to live up to its promises. Some even tasted the bitterness of what has been called CAB – Computer Assisted Bankruptcy.

In retrospect, it can be seen that the early computers were expensive, clumsy and often totally unsuited to the real world environments in which they were meant to operate.

Although the micro has helped to overcome many of the inefficiencies and limitations of earlier computers, new office technology cannot be regarded as a magic wand. If you automate an inefficient office without careful consideration it will become even more inefficient. A poorly implemented electronic system could disrupt a smoothly running and efficient operation.

Organisations can quickly become as dependent on computing power as on electric power. A microcomputer or word processor may cost a fraction of the equivalent system in the 1960s, but it can still represent a significant investment for a small company or group. If the system goes wrong, the consequences can be serious.

To avoid the pitfalls that could lie along the road to the electronic office, the technology must be kept under control. Technology is an aid, a tool. It is not a god and the high priests of technology must not be obeyed without question.

Each office, each work place, each organisation has its own special needs. There are therefore no universal rules that can be applied to every circumstance to achieve success with new office technology. This chapter and the next, however, offer some advice and useful hints, gleaned from practical experience, which could be applied to your situation.

Who's in charge?

If you run a very small business or group, or are looking for a microcomputer or word processor for your own use, there is no argument about who is in charge of decisions about how to use new technology.

In larger organisations, decisions about the electronic office fit into the general management style. Some organisations have a strict top-down hierarchy in which managers take decisions more or less on their own, with little consultation. In others, there is a considerable degree of industrial democracy in which all levels of staff participate in decision-making.

There are lessons from past experiences of computer-based systems that should be born in mind.

The first is that computer professionals should *not* be allowed to take charge. During the 1960s and 70s, a cadre of computing experts grew up in data processing departments. Their expertise, and to some extent their loyalties, lay in computing rather than in the mainstream work of the organisation. Lack of technical understanding amongst managers and users often means that the computing people effectively shape the way the system works and, therefore, the kinds of jobs and working methods that flow from the new system.

This leads to one of the most frequent faults with computer services – a failure to take account of the real world needs of users and operators. Remote from the daily life of the organisation, the computing professionals build systems that give more prominence to theoretical 'logical' information needs than to the way people actually work.

The second lesson, which follows from the first, is that the people who are most affected by the new system, whose jobs depend on the way the electronic office operates, should have some influence on the form it takes. This participation should be more than just being interviewed by technical designers and analysts.

Even in organisations where managers jealously guard their 'right to manage', it would be a mistake, for example, to buy a word processor without having it evaluated by secretarial staff. Involvement of users should mean that the final system is closer to actual user requirements.

The third lesson is that all levels of staff are more positively motivated to use the technology effectively if they are kept informed about plans for technological innovation. Secrecy can lead to suspicion and fear, which can erupt into various forms of resistance. Middle managers and adminstrators, as well as secretarial and clerical staff, often complain that they have been left in the dark about new computing and electronic office developments.

Facts, fudges and fantasies

Any innovation involves an element of risk. The electronic office is a major innovation in working life, so the outcome is bound to be unpredictable. Yet many managers demand detailed, quantified 'proofs' of the costs and benefits of a new system, before they agree to invest in one.

Many *cost/benefit analyses* are little more than reasonable guesstimates. Yet they can cast a shadow on the whole project although they focus on narrow and misleading measurements. When the system is eventually installed and running, it may be judged purely on the grounds of the original cost/benefit targets, however misguided they were. False goals may then be worshipped, while ignoring other important potential benefits.

At one conference on new office technology, a manager in the audience commented: 'I am convinced that the electronic office will be of great value to my department. But how do I produce figures to convince my senior managers when I cannot be sure of exactly what will happen when we install new systems?' The answer from a leading consultant was crisp: 'Think of a number. Say you will increase typing productivity by that percentage. Then make sure you are not around when that figure has to be justified!'

That cynical quip is a comment on what often occurs. 'Typing productivity' is a typical thing to attempt to quantify. It is relatively easy to work out that one typist can produce $x\%$ more typing with a word processor than an electric typewriter (figures of 600% and more have been bandied about but 60% to 200% is more realistic, depending on the type of work being done). As the amount that can be invested in new equipment sometimes depends on such figures, there can be a tendency to fudge the figures to make them look as good as possible.

Cost-substitution arguments can then be developed which go something like this: 'Increased productivity means that fewer typists can do more work. We can therefore pay for new word processors by cutting the number of typists. We will substitute lower technology costs in place of higher people costs.'

Of course, word processors do produce productivity improvements in most cases. Their true value, however, may be difficult to determine.

Typing throughput may improve but some of the increase may be wasted. 'Principals' who originate material often get text changed unnecessarily just because it is easy to do so on a word processor. If word processing work is organised in a way that is detrimental to the overall support given to managers, the improvements in typing may be offset by inefficient use of managers' time.

In any case, typing may only take up 50% or less of the time of secretaries and clerical staff. As secretaries and clerks comprise typically less than 15% of office staff costs, gains in typing productivity may not be of such general significance.

By emphasising typing productivity, the word processor tends to become used as a typewriter replacement. For this purpose, an electronic typewriter can often be sufficient. Word processors have a richness of capability far wider than the typing aspect. Too often, much of this power is left untapped.

Something ventured, something gained

The cost-substitution approach lacks vision. It tends to examine short-term economic and technical questions because they are the factors most easily quantified. It is essentially negative and backward looking. 'How do I do what I am doing cheaper?' is the basic question.

A more positive and imaginative approach to the consequences of office innovation is to ask what the system can *add*: how it can *improve* the way the organisation is run; *extend* the services or products provided; *enhance* the jobs and working environment of all staff. This *value-added* method enlarges the horizons for new systems. Cost-substitution calculations should play a role within such broader considerations.

Typing tasks, for example, should be just one of the range of word processing facilities evaluated. Explorations should also be made of how word processors and associated systems may influence the way the organisation operates, offer opportunities for completely new services, and change office jobs, personnel and training policies, and many other key social, organisational and long-term economic aspects.

At some point, of course, a study has to be made of the immediate costs of implementing a system and some targets set as a basis for assessing how well the system is working once it is operational.

It is important that more is added to the 'costs' side of the cost-benefit balance than just the price of the hardware and software. Support and maintenance for the equipment, staff training, conversion from the current ways of working, changes to office buildings, new furniture, and other costs must not be forgotten.

A variety of factors should also be placed in the benefits scales. Weighting should be given to qualitative as well as quantitative gains – better customer service, improved quality of information on which to make decisions, happier and more motivated staff, and so on.

When the time comes, a decision to go ahead with any new aspects of the electronic office must have its dash of faith, hope and clarity of purpose. The key to many successful electronic office changes has been top managers who *first* decide that new office technology is to be used in some way *then* give the go-ahead to find out the best way of doing it.

Experience is the best teacher

Nothing ventured, nothing gained is an apt cliché in this context. It is also true that something ventured, something risked. An office technology project is likely to have uncertainties and disappointments, as well as promise and achievement.

Until you and your colleagues get your hands on electronic office systems and try them in a working environment, you will not be able to realise what new opportunities arise, as well as what problems exist. Most people and organisations approach new technology tentatively at first. Only its most obvious and easy to use features are activated. Progress in doing new things with the system is relatively slow during the first phase.

As experience is gained, users begin to feel more confident. They start to see the potential for doing new things. Then the pace rapidly quickens as they shoot up the *learning curve*, seeking to extend and enhance the system. As demand rises, the problem becomes how to satisfy that demand in a co-ordinated way without inhibiting grassroots initiatives.

Such learning-by-experience must be expected and planned for. It should be recognised that the future is uncertain, so systems should be developed with as much inbuilt flexibility as possible to enable them to adapt to change. Uncertainty also means that mistakes are likely to happen, particularly in the early, tentative phases.

Failure should also be anticipated and handled openly. People should be allowed to make mistakes while they are learning without the fear that they will always be criticised and disciplined. New systems should never be placed immediately at the heart of an organisation's operations, where failure could have serious impact and leave scars that could take a long time to heal.

Pilot projects can help in the first stages of an electronic office. They should be in a self-contained activity, say a new service, which is not critical to the main functioning of the organisation. Lessons can be learnt from the pilot before moving to more significant activities.

In many circumstances, it would probably be advisable to run a new system alongside the old methods for a time. Money spent in such *parallel* operations should be seen as an insurance against putting all your eggs in an electronic basket too quickly, then finding the basket collapses.

Getting into a virtuous circle

Computers are powerful, logical and complex beasts. They cannot be handled in a haphazard, easy-going way or else they bite. They need careful, considerate, sensitive and systematic handling when they are to be applied to any serious work.

You need an action plan and a strategy whether you are looking for the simplest micro or for a complete electronic office. The task of selecting a system is not like choosing a new electric typewriter or calculator. It is a continuing process that should include the 10 steps shown below.

1 Establish what you want to achieve.
2 Find out what the technology can do for you.
3 Explore what needs to be done and the feasibility of doing it.
4 Evaluate alternatives.
5 Choose the most appropriate option.
6 Design or buy/rent system.
7 Implement and run it.
8 Continually monitor and assess the system in action.
9 Learn from experience.
10 Revise what you want to achieve.

When laid out as a list, these ten steps to electronic paradise seem to suggest that you proceed through them in a clean-cut, logical progression. Real life is rarely like this. It is more muddled, with many things going on at once.

To start with, there is the chicken-and-egg problem inherent in the first two steps Which comes first? Deciding what you want to achieve, or finding out what the technology can do (which might give you new ideas about what you want to achieve)? The answer is that you will have to do a bit of both at the same time.

Similarly, while you are exploring what needs to be done, you will inevitably be assessing alternative ways of doing it. The whole thing eventually loops around on itself because what you learn from experience will change what you want to achieve, so the cycle begins again.

It is better to think of these stages as a circle, where there is continuous interaction between each stage. It is like a living, evolving creature which grows with experience, even if progress often goes in fits and starts and may wander down blind alleys at times.

Shooting at moving targets

Computer consultants love to talk about 'setting objectives.' 'Before you look for a system, decide on your objectives,' is a typical piece of advice. It tends to assume that people and organisations can pinpoint exactly what they are aiming to do. In practice, there are often many targets, some conflicting with each other, some neat and tidy, with easily quantifiable objectives, others fuzzy and difficult to define precisely.

The future is a set of moving targets. In order to have any chance of hitting them, there are two golden rules to follow. Firstly, *plan long but act promptly*. Secondly, bring to the surface as many targets as possible from the beginning.

A *strategic plan* is needed to map out where you are going in the long term. Prompt *tactical* action is needed to move the thing along. Although it is true that developments will probably go at an evolutionary rate, you should not sit back and wait.

While the strategy should change relatively slowly, tactics can be altered quickly if the project is going off course. Without strategic guidelines, however, tactical mistakes can prove disastrous.

For example, a typical strategic goal is to have an electronic office that is sufficiently flexible to adapt to the inevitable changes that occur in the way organisations operate and work is carried out. At a tactical level, this means that when choosing specific systems, priority must be given to checking whether the system not only meets today's needs but can expand and be linked to other systems.

The strategy should bring to the fore a broad range of objectives, not just the technical and short-term economic targets favoured in cost-substitution approaches. Explicit aims should be set out covering human and organisational aspects. Designing a computer-based system also means designing new jobs, new working procedures, new organisational structures, new management techniques

A new system should work well not only when it is first installed but throughout its working life. It must be maintained, serviced, corrected, enhanced and developed. New services may grow from the technology, new jobs may be created, new skills needed.

When assessing how well the system is operating once it is running, those initial explicit targets provide 'prompts' to avoid important things being forgotten. If, for example, one aim is to enrich jobs for staff and another is to improve 'productivity', there will be less chance that, as has sometimes happened, typing productivity has improved at the expense of creating such boring and stressful jobs that there is a massive staff turnover.

Experimenting in the 'play' room

One of the most frequent worries for someone new to information technology is often expressed like this: 'I have heard all about the wonders of the electronic office. I am sure that some of it would be useful to me and my company. But how do I find out what different systems can do for me when I am swamped in incomprehensible gobbledegook whenever I try to find out?'

This problem was more difficult to solve before the micro leapt into the public consciousness and cheap microcomputers were bought for homes and schools. The best way of understanding what the systems can do for you is to use them and play with them.

Some organisations have helped their staff by setting up electronic workshops or 'play' rooms. Here, people can come to try out micros, word processors and terminals in a relaxed atmosphere. With some Computer Assisted Learning software and computer games, people can find out for themselves how to operate systems and to feel confident with them.

Many executives, for example, feel that sitting at a keyboard is beneath them. They are also frightened of being seen to be clumsy and make mistakes in front of their staff.

As well as the informal 'out of sight' experience gained in a workshop, executives can find help from an 'information centre', as used by the assistant manager in Chapter 2. This offers an 'open house' where managers can learn about the things that the electronic office can do for them in live working situations.

Having a home computer, even if it is used mainly for playing games, can help to crack the myth that computing is difficult and only for specialists. Education in the use of computing systems is becoming commonplace in schools, colleges, universities and adult education institutes.

Of course, there are books (like this one), magazines, articles in newspapers, TV programmes (like the BBC's Computer Literacy series), radio features and other information that will help to explain what the electronic office can do for you. Suppliers of systems will also be eager to let you have brochures and guides that can be informative if you ignore the sales spiel.

You should also talk to friends and other contacts who have actually used systems. They can tell you what systems have been like in practice, the joys and the tears, the disappointments and surprises.

Getting down to the nitty gritty

The preliminaries discussed so far are important to the ultimate success of an electronic office project – deciding why technology is being introduced, setting targets, and so on. At some point, however, the nitty gritty *Where? What? How?* and *When?* questions must be asked and answered.

Where and when is the new system to be introduced? What is it going to do? How is it to be done? When will it be implemented? In a large project, answering these questions can lead to the full palaver of a *feasibility study*. For even a small system, however, a systematic study should be made.

The current way of working needs to be analysed. A picture then needs to be built up of how things might be once new systems are installed. Then choices have to be made about what can be achieved in practice.

Economic issues to be studied include: where current costs arise; the price of current inefficiencies (lost invoices, out-of-date information to work with, clients kept waiting for welfare payments, orders lost, etc); the cost of failure once the system is installed and what to pay in terms of having stand-by systems and reliable and prompt servicing and repair; financial benefits that may be achieved with new systems; costs of training, transferring old files into computer form, translating software from one machine to another, and so on.

Social aspects of how the organisation runs and people work must be carefully examined. What working rules and procedures have been laid down and how do people actually behave? Who is responsible for various functions? How does management get information about what is going on? Who reports to whom? What divisions, departments, teams exist? Are there any important informal cliques or groups?

Then there are questions about individual jobs. What tasks are being performed? How are these tasks formed into job descriptions? What do staff like and dislike about existing jobs? What skills do staff have? What new skills are needed? Do personnel policies allow sufficient mobility to cope with future changes?

Technical issues cover factors that can be more easily quantified, like the volume of information being handled; the types of transaction task carried out (answering a query, recording an order, updating a file, etc); response times needed for particular tasks; the numbers of files and items within those files; and so on.

For word processing, factors to be considered include the lengths and types of documents produced; in what form documents originate (dictation, handwriting, from other workstations, etc); locations where principals originate text; average numbers of copies per memo; and many others.

All this clearly involves a lot of work. Experience is needed (or experts should be called in to help) to handle the kinds of formal diagnosis techniques needed to dig out the information and to produce detailed specifications needed to design and select particular systems.

Grapevines around the tea lady

Within any organisation there is usually a manual which contains the rules governing the way an office should formally operate. Few offices stick to the rule book. Office work is often unpredictable. Office staff like to have their own ways of doing things. Managers like to build up their own relationships with their local staff.

Managers down the line sometimes use a touch of 'creative insurgency' to water down or deflect edicts from above that may make sense elsewhere in the organisation but would cause problems locally. They may turn a blind eye to some staff breaking formal rules, or even bend the rules themselves.

This informal way of working can give the local manager a considerable degree of autonomy over her or his local workplace. Through give-and-take discussions, negotiations and bargaining (other than formal labour relations procedures), compromises are reached which oil the wheels of office activity.

Decisions are often made on the basis of informal chats rather than via formal reporting mechanisms. Memos and copies of memos are frequently sent as part of the game of office politics. People are reluctant to commit to paper their doubts, anger, criticism, proposals for the future, and other key feelings and actions until they have been discussed informally, sometimes secretively.

Everyone who has worked in an office knows the effectiveness of the gossip grapevine in passing information. All office workers have experienced times when they have picked up some vital piece of information while standing in a queue for a tea lady or vending machine, walking into a colleague's office for a chat, or

talking over a drink. Equally, it is common to sit through long meetings which are meant to be the forum for exchanging information but learn absolutely nothing because the truth is being hidden and personal power games are being waged instead.

One of the gravest potential dangers of the electronic office is that it could disrupt and destroy crucial informal practices and ways of working life. Rules and procedures can be programmed into software so that deviations will not be allowed or will be reported automatically to higher authority. This can be done in regard to management decision making as well as to the routines that need to be followed by junior clerks.

As more information flows through electronic mail, which can be timed and recorded accurately, so the opportunities could diminish for informal but effective communications. The electronic office can act like an X-ray machine, making organisational procedures and information visible to those with a licence to look.

Such *transparency* could act like a straightjacket on the way the organisation acts, stifling individual initiative. Of course, human ingenuity will find ways round the system and set up new informal channels. These are likely to be more limited than in the past because the formal system can tighten its grip through computer control.

Failure to understand the importance of the difference between formal and informal office methods has been a major cause of failure in many computer-based systems.

Central control or local autonomy?

The size, cost and limited capability of early large computers in the 1960s meant that they were best suited for organisations with centralised power structures. Now chips have made decentralised computing a reality. This does not mean, however, that new systems will inevitably be used as part of a process of moving power and decision making away from the centre.

New office technology can be used either to reinforce central control or to provide the mechanism for implementing an efficient form of local decentralisation. A workstation, for example, can be used for purely personal work. It can also act as part of a local group or department. And it can be plugged into central information networks and databases.

This interconnection can be used by senior management to control and monitor all work and to severely restrict the leeway allowed for individual discretion and initiative. Those who believe in this centralised approach argue that it creates a more disciplined and efficient working method, reducing errors and misjudgements caused by allowing individuals to do their own thing too much.

On the other hand, distributed computing can be used as a vehicle for giving a great deal of autonomy to local groups within a co-ordinated framework and to provide the advantages of large-scale planning without stifling invaluable local initiatives. This is true for private business and public administration.

Introducing new office technology is essentially a political process (with a small 'p'). It often leads to vigorous management in-fighting. New systems cut across traditional management boundaries and threaten to undermine little empires built by managers. Control of electronic office developments is seen as an important lever in these power battles, so there is likely to be a battle between various executives, office administrators, data processing professionals and others to take charge of electronic office projects.

Technological change raises fundamental questions about authority and democracy. Who decides? What values are to be used in judgements – purely questions of 'efficiency' or should some priority also be given to 'social' factors like job satisfaction? Who participates in decision making? Is information about change to be made freely available or kept within a small group? Who benefits from the technology? Who pays?

Choosing and implementing an electronic office system is therefore not just a technical matter. It is part of the muscle and lifeblood that drives the organisation.

What to do and when

There are so many ways in which electronic systems can be used that it can be difficult to decide what to do first and when to bring in other services. Again, the best approach is the evo-revolutionary formula: plan long, act short.

There should be a carefully phased, step-by-step plan of how the system is to be introduced and when various functions will be added on. As far as possible, each step should be self-contained, so that if something goes wrong, the poison doesn't spread. When problems arise, lessons can be learnt and the plan modified accordingly.

When examining the various information tasks carried out in an organisation, a level of priority should be assigned to the most significant. The tasks that most influence the operation of the organisation should be the ones that most influence the electronic system.

The most potentially disastrous course to follow is to try to integrate all applications into the same system from day one. Attempts to do this caused much Computer Assisted Bankruptcy in the 1960s and 70s. The complexity of trying to do everything at once creates a tangled web that produces only knots.

The kit approach

In systems design jargon, a *structured, modular* approach is the best to adopt. 'Structured' means providing a framework, a strategic plan that keeps all elements of the system in perspective and going in the same direction. A 'module' is any self-contained unit that has interactions with other modules in the overall system. They enable work to carry on in digestible bites.

Modular methods help to isolate problems and avoid general contamination from one rotten module. They also promote considerable flexibility and adaptability. Modules can be added or taken away to change the shape of a system without always requiring a complete re-design. If one or more modules fail, it may be possible for the rest of the system to operate at reduced performance. This is picturesquely known as *graceful degradation*.

The structured framework is vitally important. If this goes wrong, modules will not fit together and the whole thing could collapse or at least a lot of effort will be needed to link modules.

A structured, modular technique can be applied to the overall strategy and to detailed designs of hardware and software. In software development, *structured design* and *structured programming* methods have belatedly instilled some engineering discipline to replace what had previously been a haphazard, unreliable art form.

The main thrust of the implementation strategy should be towards those information handling tasks central to the organisation's effectiveness. As has been said earlier, however, it is probably better to try out a pilot project or two in less sensitive areas to get an understanding of how the system works before going live on the main system.

Remember always to consider the cost of failure: what happens if the system goes wrong. Besides all other costs caused by disruption to office work, if the early systems are highly visible throughout the organisation and something goes wrong, attitudes to any future developments can be soured. The 'blame the computer' syndrome which spread after early computer failures has cast a long shadow that still darkens some peoples' view of any computer-based system.

Squeeze the fruit before eating

From the feasibility studies, a rough sketch should begin to emerge of the size, shape and cost of the new system. Before filling in the details of that sketch so that it forms a precise specification for the final system, various alternative organisations, job and systems designs should be considered.

There are a number of ways of designing an organisation. For example, in an *hierarchical* management structure, each person has one superior (except the chief executive at the top). A *matrix management* approach, however, has one person reporting to different managers on different projects.

The introduction of new office technology can be an opportunity to re-evaluate how the organisation is managed and the ways in which information is gathered and exchanged. Various possibilities are also opened up for designing the types of jobs people do, which are examined fully in the next chapter.

Before opting for a particular hardware and software solution, consideration should be given to the general type of system needed, such as whether a word processor, general-purpose microcomputer or multi-function workstation is best; whether a central system with terminals or distributed processing is more suitable; or whether stand-alone or shared resources systems are most appropriate.

Taking a lesson from the street market, the sweetness of results can best be judged by having a squeeze before deciding to buy. The people who will have to live with the system should be given the chance of trying out alternatives either at a supplier's demonstration centre or through an onsite trial. It could be money well spent (if the outlay is not too great) to obtain one or two systems purely on an experimental basis.

Users who have already bitten should be asked what the taste is like. Their circumstances are likely to differ from your own in some way but may still be relevant. Be on your guard, however, against a user who is a 'plant' for the supplier, who has given him a special deal so that he will act as a *reference sell* (the marketing jargon) to say how good their products are. Find out if there are *user groups* for a particular system or application in which you are interested.

When evaluating systems, you should always refer back to the original targets you set. As these should comprehensively cover economic, human, organisational and technical matters, they should keep the final decisions on course with the strategic plan.

Also, always bear in mind that the purpose of the exercise is not just to choose pieces of equipment and slabs of software. Many organisations have found that the process of looking at the way they work from a fresh and systematic viewpoint is in itself a way of making many improvements that are not directly related to new equipment.

In some cases, the results of feasibility investigations may be to recommend new working methods without getting any new technology, at least in the short term.

The tender trap

When it is reasonably clear what is needed, a *tender* proposal can be drawn up. This should clearly state the performance expected; the volumes and types of information to be handled; the support that will be required from the supplier (training, servicing, bug-correction, etc); and other information about the supplier's business, such as its experience and financial stability, how many users there are of similar systems, how many servicing centres and software and hardware maintenance engineers, and so on.

If you are just interested in a microcomputer, you can take this tender around with you when you go to dealer showrooms to see what is on offer. Otherwise, an *invitation to tender* can be sent to likely suppliers or, in the case of large systems, advertised in relevant publications.

From here on, the suppliers can lay many traps for the unwary and inexperienced. You should therefore get as much training yourself beforehand and also take the advice of experts who know the ropes. If you are in an organisation with is own DP and technical systems professionals, get them to help you. They probably bear the scars of previous experiences so will know the warning signs to look out for.

There are *consultancies* and advisory centres who hire their specialists out, usually on a daily rate. Some provide special deals for smaller companies. A good consultant will be like a good accountant: she or he will save you far more money than you pay for their services, although you may initially gasp when you hear their fees.

You should be as careful in choosing a consultant as selecting a supplier. Check their track record, their strengths and weaknesses. Try to talk to people who have acted on their advice.

Just as computer experts talk in technical jargon, so many consultants lapse into 'consultantese'. This is designed to sound good and to fill out reports. Often it masks bland waffle. So get them to explain themselves crisply and clearly. With larger consultancy firms, write into the contract that if the quality of a consultant working with you is not up to expectations, you can have him or her replaced. Some firms surf on the waves of the reputations built up by their senior staff, although some of the people working for them may not be that good.

Coping with option shock

The value of doing your groundwork at the start will become evident when dealing with potential suppliers. You will be bombarded with different solutions, each of them sounding reasonable. You will find yourself suffering from *option shock*: having too much choice, with new products and services appearing too rapidly for anyone to keep pace with them.

A systematic, structured framework – strategic plans, social, economic and technical objectives, and all that jazz – provides the ring of confidence needed to hold your nerve, to insist on hitting *your* targets.

You will probably find that the solutions pushed by different suppliers (and, unfortunately, by some consultants) derive from *their* past experience and the technologies *they* are comfortable with, and are not necessarily what is best for you.

A company with a primarily office equipment background, for example, will often push word processing as the most important thing under the electronic sun. A company rooted in traditional data processing will stress the virtues of general purpose computers, although they may be tarted up with an 'office automation' label.

A supplier of telephone exchanges and equipment will emphasise the advantages of communications and building up systems on the basis of the existing telephone network. New companies created expressly for the electronic office will promote the wonders of 'integrated' solutions and local area networks.

The companies may genuinely believe what they are saying because they perceive the electronic office from the vantage point of their own know-how and expertise. There is nothing intrinsically wrong with any of these approaches. Equally, none is so universally superior that it should automatically start as odds-on favourite.

Option shock applies all along the line, from the overall design of the office to specific items of equipment. For instance, is it best to get a dedicated word processor, a personal micro-computer, or a networked workstation?

The answers will be found in the feasibility studies. If the most important information activity in a company or local unit is text processing, requiring a lot of word processing, then dedicated word processors would get a bonus rating. Where the main tasks are electronic mail and aids to decision support, then personal computers or executive workstations are probably better.

A workstation can either have all its functions integrated into the same software, as was used by the managing director in Chapter 2, or it may need separate programs for word processing, spreadsheets, file handling, and so on. A feasibility study should look at the costs of the systems and the degree of inconvenience involved in switching between separate functions.

Price tags can sting

There is always a temptation to go for systems with the lowest visible price tag. In cost-substitution equations, a cheap system can seem to be particularly impressive. You should be extremely cautious about such a simplistic attitude.

The immediate price may hide a whole lot of other costs. It may have been kept low because the manufacturer or dealer has skimped on quality or service provided. As soon as something goes wrong, you have to start shelling out to get it fixed.

Training and documentation may be poor, leading to a lot of time and money spent teaching people how to use the system. In addition, there are the costs and inefficiencies involved in running systems during a prolonged training period.

You may find that you get the 'as advertised' system for the promised low cost. Then in order to make the system do any sensible work you have to add disks, printers and software which push up the price significantly.

An expensive price tag can be as misleading as a cheap one. Hardware prices keep tumbling, thanks to the chip, so more costly hardware could mean the system is a bit out of date if it reflects the price of hardware at the time of its manufacture. Micro software is a mass marketing business with very low prices for some excellent software. A high software charge can indicate that it is more expensive primarily because it is available on a system with relatively few users, rather than it is of particularly high quality.

There is no short-cut to finding a 'best buy'. The systematic, sensitive and careful methods recommended in this chapter should not be bypassed.

'It meets the standard but. . . .'

The problem of incompatibilities between programming languages, software, information files, and terminals has already been mentioned. Suppliers are well aware of the desire of users to obtain systems that allow as much flexibility as possible. So they will often claim that features 'meet the standard', even when they are stretching the truth.

Some standards arise because a system becomes very popular. The operating system CP/M, developed by Digital Research of the US, became such a *de facto* standard on early micro-computers. This was a considerable aid to users because developers of software could design their systems to run under CP/M rather than particular makes of micro.

In practice, however, because the machine code and structure of proceessors vary, CP/M is not always implemented in the same way on different machines. Software that runs under CP/M on one machine may not work under the CP/M of another machine.

You can also find that two programs which run separately on a machine give problems when you try to link information between them. For example, you may wish to apply a word processor program to the information created by file management systems. Even if such links have been made under CP/M on another system, you can have difficulties on yours because of the way the 'underware' on your CP/M handles the information.

With a de facto standard, rather than one agreed through national and international bodies, there is the probability that it won't last. For example, there are now many other operating systems like Unix, MS-DOS, Pick and others that have become extremely popular.

There are similar problems with standardisation of storage media both in terms of physical characteristics, like size, and the way information is recorded. Exchanging files and applications betweem systems can founder on the rocks of incompatibility.

Nothing about compatibility should be left to chance. You should check any claims about having 'standard' systems. Warning bells should ring if any such claims are qualified with an 'except for a few minor differences.' With computing standards, the exception *does not* prove the rule.

They who hesitate

One of the fears about buying a system is that a better bargain may appear tomorrow. Like Mr Micawber in Charles Dickens' *David Copperfield*, 'in case something turned up,' is the favourite expression of many people sitting on the electronic office fence.

Such Micawberism is fully justified in the sense that, almost inevitably, something better, faster, cheaper is likely to appear from some supplier tomorrow. That is a result of rapid technological progress and the sharp competitiveness of the market.

This does not mean, however, that hesitation is a good policy. As the credo of this chapter has emphasised: plan long, act short. You can go on waiting for ever if you are obsessed with the fear of missing a bargain.

Provided you have been through the correct procedures in deciding what you want and finding a system that does it, you should not hesitate. While you wait for something better, you will be missing the benefits of using the system, which will probably be far more important than any advantages gained by waiting for something else to turn up.

A valid reason for a delay is if there is some important gap in the systems currently available which is of significance to the task being carried out. You may need, for example, voice or handwriting input but find that existing products are too expensive, unreliable or limited.

Take care with the newborn Jaws

Another reason for not continually chasing the newest system is that computer-based systems are notorious for having teething troubles. In some cases the 'teething problems' have been so vicious that users may think they have been savaged by the shark from *Jaws*.

Much of the advice earlier in this chapter can lead you to go for tried and proven systems. A new system has no other users you can talk to about how it works. A new system will probably have some software bugs, possibly some hardware problems.

With a new system, you often find that all promised features are 'not available in the current release' and so you wait some time to get what you want. New systems often exhibit problems when attempts are made to do something that has not been done before.

Suppliers have even announced 'paper tiger' systems that exist in prototype form (or just on the drawing board) but have not yet been tested in a real working environment.

Of course, some people must try out new systems, otherwise innovations will dry up. Suppliers often give special deals with new products, like providing extra support to their 'guinea pig' users so that they can get live experience of the system and build up a base of customers and reference sells.

In some circumstances, you may feel that a newborn electronic office system is what you want. You should go into such deals with your eyes open and not be surprised if the young one uses you to get over its teething troubles.

Loose ends that can trip you up

This chapter has covered a lot of ground but it has still only scratched the surface of what users have to consider and do in order to control the way the electronic office develops. Some things which eventually turn out to be of major importance might appear at first to be relatively minor.

For example, questions about the building and office furniture may not seem to be problems in such a 'hi-tech' arena. In fact, they are crucial. Electronic office equipment needs a lot of special cabling, ventilation and other environmental considerations. Ergonomic and health and safety requirements also affect the physical environment, as described in the next chapter.

Space will need to be found, and special storage equipment obtained, for disks and tapes. The siting of electronic office equipment is important, so alterations may have to be made to rooms.

If environmental factors are considered too late in the day, there can be a lot of extra cost and disruption. It has been known for building changes and office furniture to cost as much, if not more, than all the new electronic hardware and software.

Then there is the question of back-up in case something goes wrong. A secure area will need to be found to store copies of disks and tapes containing older information which can be used to re-create an information base if something goes wrong with the live information.

Some kind of arrangement also needs to be made to guard against major system failures. This can mean choosing a system of *high resilience*, which has a great deal of duplicate equipment and fails with graceful degradation. Arrangements should be made with the supplier and other users to run your programs on similar systems to your own in emergencies. Stand-by generators may also be needed.

Overall security procedures in the organisation should be re-examined. Privacy of information in the system needs to be protected through software control and the physical protection of terminals and storage.

Insurance must also be taken out. While this is relatively easy for the hardware, it is more difficult to assess damage caused by serious disruption to the system or loss of information. Insurance companies may want evidence of the security and back-up precautions that have been taken.

Negotiating the contract

The last stage in a selection process is to negotiate and sign the contract with a supplier. This should be done with the utmost care.

If there is a significant problem with the system or the service given by the supplier, you could want compensation. This will be difficult to get unless you have included in the contract clear and unambiguous statements of the performance you expect and where responsibility lies for achieving it.

Suppliers usually have a standard contract that they like you to sign. Naturally, this is designed to favour them as much as possible. Before signing anything, check it out with a legal expert or with someone experienced in electronic office systems.

The types of things you can reasonably expect to find in a contract include the *availability* of the system; the percentage of time the system is available for use: response times at terminals; *Mean Time Between Failure (MTBF)*, the minimum average time between failures of the system; and the speed with which service engineers will respond to urgent calls.

Before putting a system into live action, suppliers often run *benchmarks* – typical workloads that indicate the performance of the machine. Passing a bench test, even one tailored to your own requirements, is no guarantee that the system will perform to that level in live operation.

The supplier should agree in the contract to ensure that the system will carry out the functions promised in the product's specification at the time of its delivery. Functions left out until later releases of a system can cause costly delays to the organisation using the system.

The question of responsibility can be a tricky one in systems where there is more than one supplier. You can, for example, obtain a microcomputer system from a dealer in which the main computer, the printer, disk storage, and each software product comes from a different supplier.

If there is a problem, you may find yourself in the middle of a dispute between suppliers. The hardware supplier blame software faults. The applications software supplier blames the operating system, and vice versa. The dealer denies any responsibility for anything.

It is before you sign the contract that you should clarify who is responsible, what is expected and what happens if there is a dispute. Even the best laid plans can go wrong.

A chameleon technology

This chapter has shown that the design, development, selection and implementation of electronic office systems seeps into every aspect of office life. The technology provides a lot of options and a great deal of flexibility. It can be moulded to many different organisational shapes.

It is often said that technology is a neutral force that cannot be regarded as intrinsically 'good' or 'bad'. This is true, but the way technology is used reflects the values and power structures within the organisations using it as well as in society as a whole.

Computer-based systems are a particularly chameleon-like technology. They take on the attitudes of the people who design them and program them. They can re-inforce autocratic central-ised control or encourage local democracy.

If the people who are in charge of electronic office systems wish it to be so, the technology can make office jobs more varied, more enjoyable, more rewarding. On the other hand, its pro-grammed nature means that computing easily lends itself to be used to turn office work into the pressurised, monotonous, stressful jobs common to manufacturing production lines.

The next chapter looks at the factors that are likely to shape office jobs in the future.

5   The shape of office jobs to come

Robots made of flesh and blood

A world ruled by computer-controlled robots. That is one image of the future presented by science fiction writers. It is still a fantasy, despite the veneer of cleverness displayed by computers and robots.

There is a more immediate possibility: people turning into flesh and blood robots. People could become so dependent on computers that they forget how to think for themselves. Jobs could be so automated that people are expected to work like automatons or machine minders.

The fear of people becoming cogs in an automated machine pre-dates computers. Charlie Chaplin's film *Modern Times*, released in 1938, graphically illustrates how people could be regarded as components of manufacturing mechanisation; human modules that can be replaced one day by more 'reliable', less strike-prone automated units.

If the electronic office is regarded primarily in terms of *automating* work, the philosophy of production line mechanisation may become common in office work. Many jobs could then become highly routinised, strictly following the rules pre-programmed into the system and continually paced and monitored by computer.

As indicated in Chapter 2, computers can also be an aid to the enhancement of office jobs, reducing drudgery, providing new career opportunities and generally improving office life from a human point of view. Similar gains in efficiency and effectiveness can be made from either *office automation* or *computer-aided office work* approaches.

Taylor-made for Fords

The 'Modern Times' techniques of production automation were derived from the work of an American engineer, Frederick Winslow Taylor, in the late nineteenth century. His *scientific management* methods, often known as Taylorism, were applied by Henry Ford when he built the first Ford motor car assembly plant in Michigan in 1914.

Taylorism has subsequently been highly influential in designing jobs, particularly in manufacturing industries. It has also been taken onboard, usually unknowingly, by technical systems analysts when developing computer-based information systems.

The basic theory of Taylorism is that managers should use 'rational intelligence' and 'scientific' analysis to define how work should be carried out. The objective is to achieve maximum profitability for the organisation and to dangle the carrot of increased earnings as an incentive for workers to continually increase their work rate.

Taylor broke each job into its 'logical' component actions. He used a stop watch to measure how long it look to carry out each task. Then he analysed how the operating units could be re-organised and the time taken to do each task speeded up to improve overall efficiency.

Such 'time and motion' methods were instilled into production jobs. So were Taylor's underlying philosophy and view of the roles of management and workers. He believed managers should be 'thinkers' and 'planners', and workers should be 'doers'. The manager's duty in this role is to set specific targets; the worker's is to achieve them and be rewarded.

According to Taylorism, the 'scientific' solution chosen by managers should not rely too much on the most unpredictable elements in it – the people doing the work. Jobs were therefore divided into small, isolated units, each requiring a limited range of skills and allowing the worker little choice to deviate from his or her pre-determined tasks.

Jobs fit for machines

Jobs defined on scientific management lines are often monotonous, requiring the frequent repetition of simple tasks. They are created more for obedient machines than for skilful and imaginative people. It is therefore not surprising that people in manufacturing industries can be replaced relatively easily by robots. Robots are ideally suited to repeating the same task endlessly and uncomplainingly. They are not so good at jobs that depend on initiative and a variety of talents.

The term 'office automation' could imply the application of Taylorism to the electronic office. This book has preferred more neutral terms like 'electronic office' and 'new office technology', although 'office automation' is often used to cover the same area.

The roots of Taylorism lie in the *rationalism* of eighteenth century philosophers and economists like Adam Smith and Jeremy Bentham. Rationalism pictures the ideal society as one which is systematically ordered and controlled according to 'objective' analyses of what people want and how people act. It was reinforced by dazzling scientific and engineering achievements that transformed people's understanding and control of nature during, and after, the Industrial Revolution.

Charles Babbage, who invented the modern computer in the 1830s (see Chapter 8), was probably the first person to perceive that computing could be the ultimate means of implementing the 'rational' society. In 1851 he wrote that his invention provided a tool for the 'substitution of machinery, not merely for the skill of the human, but for the relief of the human intellect.'

Although most computing professionals may never have heard of Taylorism, they usually approach their work in the spirit of scientific management. They see themselves as the planners and analysts who 'objectively' probe how organisations and people should work. They quantify as much as possible. Then they program their conclusions into software, providing controls of far greater sophistication than the machines available to Taylor.

Variety is the spice of working life

Taylorism tends to give priority to the technical elements in a system, with people being expected to adapt to the solution deemed best by managers and technicians. Other approaches to management and work design aim to give a higher priority to the human factor; to promote job satisfaction as well as work efficiency; and to value the contributions that can be made by the natural 'irrational' behaviour of people.

One of the most important alternatives to Taylorism in the electronic office was discovered down a coal mine in England in 1949. The National Coal Board was investigating why there was low morale and productivity amongst miners. The research team came across a colliery in South Yorkshire with a relatively happy and efficient workforce.

This mine had a different form of work organisation to the others. Generally work was split into shifts, each responsible for a different task. There was little communication between shifts. The Yorkshire miners, however, followed a working system created in pre-mechanised days. They worked in small groups, with each group responsible for all activities on a part of the face.

The groups worked autonomously with relatively little supervision.

The Tavistock Institute in London used this mining research as a basis for developing the principles of *socio-technical* systems design. This tries to achieve a harmonious blend of social, technical and economic requirements. Work is made as satisfying as possible for the individual and steps are taken to ensure that each person contributes effectively and efficiently to the whole organisation.

Taylorism reduces work into small units and isolated tasks. Socio-technical design encourages *job enrichment* through group working and jobs with a great deal of variety. Groups are allowed a considerable degree of control over how work is organised to achieve their objectives. Machines and computers are viewed as aids to people rather than as dictators of how people work.

Other methods have been developed to achieve similar human-oriented ways of working. Behavioural psychologists A. H. Maslow and Frederick Hertzberg, for example, have contributed management techniques aimed at motivating people to fulfil their potential within many different types of management structure.

Personnel policies in many organisations have been influenced by the work of the 'humanistic' schools. By its nature, office work has tended to be more variable, more flexible, more reliant on human initiative than the assembly line. This may change in the future.

On the management/union front line

New office technology has been the trigger for strikes, work-to-rules and tension between managers and staff. The electronic office touches the nerves of an organisation. It is therefore inevitably a key labour relations issue.

Technological change during the Industrial Revolution was a major reason for the growth of trade unions. In manufacturing industry, unions generally work within the framework of Taylorism and are mainly concerned with achieving the maximum material rewards for their work, provided there is reasonable job security and a physically healthy and safe environment.

In offices, negotiations between managers and staff have tended to be more concerned with broader issues about the quality of the job. Unions, staff associations and other forms of office staff representation have sought work that is satisfying as well as reasonably paid.

Many countries in western Europe have legislation and agreements between national management and union bodies that give staff a considerable say in the quality of their working environment. In the late 1970s these began to be applied to computer-based systems, often through *new technology agreements*.

Management/union agreements governing particular pieces of technology date back long before then. New technology agreements, which originated in Norway and Sweden, take a more systematic view of unions' requirements and try to influence systems before they are installed, rather than reacting afterwards.

Some managers regard technology agreements as a positive step towards creating a framework to encourage innovation. Others regard it as an attempt to interfere with a manager's 'right to manage'.

Whatever approach is adopted to technology agreements, managers should recognise that new office technology *will* affect staff relations and personnel policies. Consideration of these must be included from the earliest stages of an electronic office project.

Technology agreements also provide an 'agenda' of issues that are central to every electronic office system – the provision of information to managers and staff; participation by managers and staff in systems design and selection; health and safety; work design; training; redundancies/redeployment of staff; career development; status and job grading; pay and conditions of employment. Even if managers do not like what unions are asking for, they should take an open-minded look at the items on the agenda.

The heart of the matter

People who work at all levels in offices have two major fears about new technology. Will it do me out of a job? And if I still have a job, will it be better or worse than the one I have got now? That is the heart of the matter.

The question of levels of employment has been examined earlier in the book. Some jobs will go, many will change, some new ones will be created. Unions would like technology agreements to establish some degree of job security. Ideally, they would like managers to guarantee that there will be no reduction in the total number of jobs. Managers are generally reluctant to concede this because one of their reasons for introducing new systems is often to increase productivity and cut staff costs.

More common ground can be found in accepting that compulsory redundancy will be avoided, even if staff lost by 'natural wastage' are not replaced. For older staff, early retirement can be offered if there is to be a reduction in staff.

Opportunities for training and retraining should be available to help staff move to new jobs. In the future, it is likely that most people will learn new skills many times in their career to cope with rapid technological change. Personnel and job grading policies should be revised to ensure that they do not restrict the greater mobility of staff. They should be able to move without having to drop to a lower grade or have an immediate loss of pay.

Unions would like technology agreements to stipulate that managers will provide full information from the start of a project and that union *technology representatives* (or *data stewards*) represent staff on technical design teams. Unions believe that such information and participation is necessary if they are to have a say in designing jobs and the quality of the working environment. They would also like the opportunity to call in their own outside consultants to challenge the views of the managers' technical experts.

Some managers fear that to give unions a say in the design of the system, armed with advanced information, is to hand them a powerful weapon of leverage in general labour relations negotiations. They also question whether unions offer the best means of representing staff views.

As discussed in the previous chapter, however, whatever mechanism is agreed on, the provision of information to all levels of staff and some participation by users of the system are important elements in successfully developing and introducing new systems. Managers would be foolish to reject such ideas just because they dislike the unions' notions of how they should be carried out.

Pre-programmed for stress

Chapter 2 illustrated what electronic office jobs might be like if sufficient attention is given to making jobs as stimulating and varied as possible. The secretary's job described in that chapter shows how some careers and job roles can be enhanced.

Electronic office systems, however, can have less desirable consequences for managers, secretaries, typists and clerks, largely depending on whether systems are introduced with a Tayloristic or more 'human' orientation. The pre-programmed nature of a computer system can dominate the person using it.

Computers are also able to continually monitor a person's performance. More jobs are therefore likely to involve responding to a computer-based system that records every action. Increased intelligence can be built into a system, requiring less intelligence to be applied by the person using it.

This can occur in managerial jobs as well as for secretarial and clerical tasks. Computers can make recommendations about what decisions managers should make, putting the manager's judgement into question if he or she deviates from the computer's. Electronic mail, electronic diaries and other management systems can push managers' work into formal, highly regulated channels.

This can put a considerable strain and pressure on people. Some VDU clerical jobs have already shown signs of this. For example, researchers at a Swedish insurance company discovered in 1979 that the stress levels of a group of clerical VDU operators were similar to the levels of bus drivers in the centre of Stockholm during rush hours.

Divisions in the office community

Just as Taylorism on the production line creates many low skilled jobs that can be relatively easily automated, so may neo-Taylorism in the office. At the same time, by removing some of the dreary office tasks and offering a new range of skills and services, a new breed of office workers may emerge with sweetly enriched office jobs.

The tendency could be towards a *polarisation* of work. Many secretarial and clerical jobs may resemble an office production line, where achieving targets will produce financial rewards but offer little interest or satisfaction in the job. Supervisors, managers and professionals, however, may have jobs bubbling with interest and variety, greatly aided by the occasional use of computers.

The de-skilled clerical jobs are likely to require the operator to spend most of the day at a VDU or word processor. Much stress is felt by operators who spend most of their time inputting information from the VDU, using virtually no skill or discretion.

The electronic office is more likely to be regarded as a boon by those with more skilled jobs who spend, say, less than half their time at a workstation or who can choose when to use a computer aid (they are sometimes known as *casual users*).

There could therefore be winners and losers in the electronic office. The winners could become separated from the office 'shop-floor', breaking down the sense of community and friendly socialising that has made office life reasonably pleasant, even for people carrying out clerical tasks that in themselves seem mundane.

The electronic office can remove the need to do much of that routine drudgery but may replace it with electronic monotony, unrelieved by the informal social contact that has traditionally mellowed office life. The most common interaction for many staff could be with a computer rather than with other people.

In such isolation, staff could become *alienated* from each other and from the organisation as a whole. They could, like Charlie Chaplin in *Modern Times*, begin to feel they are a cog in a machine over which they have no control and which has no interest in them as an individual, other than as a work-producing module.

Secretaries and managers in the melting pot

The relationship between managers and secretaries is an important part of office life. Having a personal secretary can be a status symbol. Crudely this has been expressed by some male managers as: 'You will never get a word processor with a body like my secretary.'

A competent secretary often takes on many managerial functions. The traditional attitude towards promotion of female secretaries, however, meant that they rarely moved into the management stream – even if they were more able than their bosses.

The electronic office will change managerial and secretarial jobs. With electronic mail, electronic filing, electronic everything, the 'clerical' aspects of secretarial work can be done directly from a workstation by manager or secretary. Word processing can cut down on the amount of time spent typing by secretaries (traditionally, 15% to 30% of a secretary's work has been typing).

As described in Chapter 2, some secretaries are likely to take on more supervisory and managerial duties, increasingly working independently from direct managerial supervision. Managers and secretaries may become more like co-workers, sharing responsibility.

Other secretarial jobs, however, may become part of the office automation production line, remote from direct contact with managers.

Not waving but drowning in the pool

Most secretaries and typists respond positively when moving from a manual or electric typewriter to a word processor. The typing job can be so much more pleasant taking advantage of word processing goodies.

This satisfaction could fade, however, if typing is organised in a way which isolates word processing operators from the principals who originate material and if little variation is allowed in the work tasks being carried out.

Word processing pools can become like factory units churning out more and more words under pressure. Word processing operators may then lose any enjoyment in the job and become typing automatons while managers lose important personal clerical services.

The high throughput of words and the noise of the printers has led some organisations to set up print rooms responsible for collecting and distributing all hard copy. Staff who are given little else to do but act as printer babysitters will fail to appreciate the benefits of word processing.

Once again, the nature of typing and word processing jobs in the future will be determined by choices made on how work is organised, rather than by choices of this or that piece of technology.

For example, a member of staff can be given responsibility for dealing with many aspects of the same client's work rather than having each clerk specialising in just one type of activity. Group working, such as in the executive support centre described in Chapter 2, provides a means of organising work so that boring and interesting tasks can be shared out more equitably. If word processing pools are needed, staff in them can participate in their administration, keep in close contact with managers, and develop skills to exploit software capabilities to make their jobs more interesting and satisfying.

Managers in the firing line

Middle managers and administrators are often primarily 'paper pushers' and go-betweens, filtering information upwards to senior managers and downwards to operational managers and staff.

The electronic office places information directly at the finger-tips of senior executives and opens new means of direct communication from top management to the rest of the organisation. Decision support systems can remove some of the autonomy of middle managers. Their jobs become more structured, stressful and closely observed via the electronic system.

Anxieties about how their jobs may change can create fears in managers about new technology, similar to those held by secretaries and clerks. While unions representing clerical staff may use blunt means to exhibit their resistance, such as strikes, managers may have more subtle methods available to them.

Managers frequently claim they cannot use keyboards and have to wait until suitable voice recognition input devices are available. This objection represents the tip of a much deeper iceberg of fear, just as clerical staff focused on worries about radiation from VDUs as a symbol of their doubts.

Resistance to keyboarding is primarily pyschological. Managers may think that sitting at a keyboard is a 'menial' task below their status. Subconsciously, however, it is one way in which managers put off the day they have to start using electronic systems.

The enthusiasm with which many executives have acquired their own personal computers, particularly for 'spreadsheet' modelling, has shown that motivated managers can take to a keyboard like a woodpecker to a tree trunk.

Managers who are anxious about the impact of technology on their own jobs are often in a position to decide how new office technology is introduced. They have been able to bring in word processing freely without affecting their own work. Except for personal computers, which can be regarded as primarily for private rather than corporate uses, the day can be put off when the electronic office moves into the managerial mainstream.

Managers are usually unaware they are resisting new technology. Their worries can remain hidden and allowed to fester. It is healthier to face the fact that managers must go through a period of sometimes traumatic change.

Training for the new office race

Whatever form they take, jobs in the electronic office will require new skills. Obviously, training will have to be given in how to operate the information systems and equipment. The electronic office is not going to be a replica of the existing methods in sparkling new dress. It fundamentally changes the 'information environment' in which people work and the skills needed to survive in that environment.

Once information is stored in digital electronic form, it becomes plasticine that can be moulded by software sculptors. The way the software organises the information and allows you to get at it determines how you see it and manipulate it.

In a traditional office, files have a physical presence. Information is often remembered in terms such as 'the pink letter at the front of the blue folder in the bottom drawer of the filing cabinet.' Paper files are organised in particular ways because of their physical form.

Electronic files can be represented as 'filing cabinets', 'drawers', 'folders', etc. They can also take on many other manifestations. To be exploited to the full, computerised information must break out from old notions and staff must learn to understand new file and database methods.

As discussed in Chapter 3, there are many types of query methods that can be used to search through computerised information. Staff need to learn not only specific methods of information retrieval but also how to understand and manipulate digital databases in general.

Communicating via electronic mail requires different skills and routines to communicating by letter and memo. Using a word processor to its maximum capability needs some understanding of computerised text processing techniques and not just typing and word processor operating skills. Many, many other aspects of office life will have to be freshly re-learnt.

Computers can help to ease this training. Computer Assisted Learning can be used to teach skills directly. If systems are designed to be genuinely user friendly, they should need less training than complex systems. HELP facilities, for example can advise the user when in doubt.

Engineering the human factor

Human factors engineering/ergonomics can be a life saver. At the start of the Second World War, about 5% of US Air Force pilots were being killed during training. A team of industrial psychologists and behavioural scientists found the cause was an altimeter. It gave the correct height readings but the way the information was displayed led the pilots to think they were higher than they actually were.

As it combines psychological, behavioural and technical expertise, human factors engineering gives as much consideration to 'subjective' human requirements as to 'objective' technical characteristics. The aim is to have people and technical systems acting in harmony, comfortably and effectively.

Human factors engineering has been used widely in designing products and work environments, from telephone handsets to the cockpits of aeroplanes and control rooms in power stations. It took a long time, however, to have an influence on computer-based systems.

Computer systems in the 1960s and 70s were designed mainly by computer professionals, from the basic hardware to the final user service. Many users were themselves people with computing skills or doing specialist jobs, like airline reservation staff. A considerable amount of training and support to users was provided.

Suppliers could therefore get away with providing some pretty unfriendly, difficult to use systems. Things began to change when computers became accessible through VDU terminals. Users began to get more critical of the design of systems, particularly of the hardware ergonomics.

The growing availability of electronic office systems made human factors more important. Suppliers realised that they could not sell systems unless they were 'user friendly'. Staff unions pushed vigorously for the implementation of ergonomic standards. Managers would select systems for their own use only if they were appealing. Some countries, particularly in Scandinavia and West Germany, established national ergonomic and health and safety standards.

Generally, electronic office systems are much better from a human factors point of view than their data processing predecessors. Many, however, still fall far short of genuine user friendliness. Human factors design should be of critical importance when choosing between systems.

The case of the pregnant man

When looking at a system, an important human factors consideration is the way in which a person interacts with it to carry out tasks in an office. This is known as *user/system interaction*, *software ergonomics*, and *man/machine communications*. If it goes wrong, the functioning of the office can be upset, leading to the provision of a poor service to those who expect the office to help them.

Take the case of a man in America who applied for a job. When he was rejected, he asked the Personnel Department why. A clerk looked up his computerised file. She confirmed he had been rejected but could not explain why because the computer coding for 'reasons for not getting a job' was a number which she did not understand.

After persistently trying to find out why he had failed, he eventually discovered that the numerical rejection code meant 'Pregnant'. His file had become mixed up with that of a lady with a similar name. If understandable codes had been used, not numbers, the mix up could have been easily discovered at an earlier stage.

This is an example of one principle of good human factors design. Wherever possible, the language used in the interaction should be clearly understood by the people using the system. *Humanised coding* should be used if abbreviations are needed, making the shortenings recognisible rather than just meaningless numbers.

This principal is important in the kinds of commands that the operator is expected to use. For example, to delete text, a word processing operator should be able to either press a special key with 'Delete' on it or type in a command 'Delete', 'Del' or 'D' (or the equivalent if a language other than English is used). Many word processing systems, however, have a variety of obscure codings to carry out these functions.

Messages that tell you something is wrong (*error messages*) should be meaningful, stating what is wrong and what you can do about it. Too often you just get incomprehensible abbreviations or other technical garbage. When you look it up in the manual, you may still be none the wiser.

Having full, understandable dialogues may take up more storage space but is of great value to the user. Provided flexibility is built into the original design, it is relatively easy to change the words used. Poorly planned systems, however, can make changes costly and difficult.

A friend for all reasons

The only general rule in human factors is that there are no universal rules. People differ, jobs differ, organisations differ. The aim should be to have a system that can be made-to-measure for a particular circumstance, then adjusted to fit another. Structured, modular designs, as recommended in Chapter 4, promote such flexibility.

The user/system interaction should have different levels for users with different expertise. A novice should be hand-held and allowed to plod through the system with considerable help and prompting from the software. For experienced operators, more rapid interaction is preferable.

The way you view a task through the system should match the

natural way that you expect the work to be carried out. Systems should use words and information structures that are familiar to you and which give you a 'feel' for the task being performed, like the WASTEBIN facility used by the assistant manager in Chapter 2, or databases organised as 'filing cabinets' and 'drawers'.

On the other hand, the system should allow you to move on to completely new ways of doing things in an electronic information world. Imitating the past should be a stepping stone to the future, not a straight-jacket that keeps you tied to old ways of doing things.

The system should never be ambiguous when it requests something from you. 'Do you want to store this file?', for example, could mean 'Do you want to keep the file for future reference but do not need it now?' or 'Do you no longer have any use for the file, so should it be erased?' Before taking any major irretrievable action, like erasing information, the system should ask a question to confirm your first request.

Documentation that comes with a system should be crisp, clear, understandable and with an easy-to-reference structure for information that you are likely to want to look up in a state of anxiety when you are not sure what to do.

Response times should be appropriate to the task being carried out. With word processing, *visual integrity* is helpful: what is shown on the screen should resemble as closely as possible the format of the printed hard copy. There should be *consistency* in commands, interaction and information structures when moving from one task to another or from, say, beginner to experienced level within the same task.

There is more to human factors than the kind of simplistic hardware ergonomics, like separating keyboards from screens, which some manufacturers seem to think is sufficient justification to give a 'user friendly' marketing accolade.

VDUs and your health

There have been many reports that VDUs can damage eyesight, cause miscarriages among pregnant operators, or trigger other complaints. Research has yet to find any verifiable evidence of radiation or any other direct health hazard emanating from VDUs (see chapter 7).

There is considerable evidence, however, that in certain working environments, VDU operation can lead to an increase in a number of physical and psychological complaints, such as eyestrain, neck and shoulder pains, stress, fatigue and irritability. Precautionary measures have sometimes been taken even where nothing detrimental has been proven. For example, pregnant staff have the opportunity in some organisations to ask to be taken off VDU work.

Most of the VDU operators' aches and pains are also reported by other office workers. The basic causes are to do with posture at the desk, office lighting, the degree of monotony in the work, and other characteristics which apply to any office job.

This has led to claims that VDUs have an 'all clear' on health grounds. It is a misleading claim. Just because people have also suffered on manual systems is no excuse for allowing such problems to continue or get worse. Insufficient attention has been given to working conditions in offices; more should be done in the future.

Keynotes of physical ergonomic standards

There are firm guidelines and standards on physical ergonomics which have been established by national health and safety bodies and from many studies. The keynote of all these recommendations is the same as for other human factors: flexibility and adaptability.

The screen and keyboard should be separate so that they can be positioned as comfortably as possible. The screen should be capable of being tilted up and down and rotated horizontally to be moved to the best direction for the user. The brightness of characters on the screen should be controllable. Chairs should be adjustable for height and the angle of the back rest and should be on castors so they can be rolled easily to where the user feels most at ease.

Operators should have regular eye tests because of the special visual demands of screen-based systems. Characters on the screen should be clear, legible and stable. Images are generated on the screen by shooting electrons from a Cathode Ray Tube to a phosphor coating on the inside of the screen. As the image fades quickly, it has to be continually refreshed. A *refresh rate* of at least 50 Hertz but preferably 60 Hertz (and at least 80 Hertz for black on white screens) is advisable. (*Hertz*, abbreviated to *Hz*, is a measurement of the frequency with which a signal is transmitted).

Glare from the screen should be kept low via anti-reflective treatment. The contrast between characters and the background colour should be adjustable. Light characters on a darker background (or black on white with a high refresh rate) are preferable.

Keyboards should be no higher than 30 mm and at an angle of less than 15°. Labels on keys should be meaningful. Keys should have concave, non-glare tops; special function keys (such as cursor controls) should be grouped separately and have brighter colours than the rest.

There should be plenty of desk-top space. Document holders can help avoid undesirable head or body movements when using a VDU or word processor. Noise levels should be below 55 decibels if telephones are also being used, 65 decibels otherwise. Wall colours should be chosen to take into account that a colour after-image is left in the eye after long viewing of the same colour (say, red after viewing green characters). Lighting, antistatic carpets, air conditioning and many other factors must also be considered.

Sitting all day inputting information or doing some other monotonous task at a VDU can be tiring to the eye and mind. Many organisations have therefore agreed to allow operators to have *rest periods* after a spell at the VDUs. Technology agreements have specified rest periods that vary from 10 minutes after every 50 minutes, to 30 minutes after every two hours.

The most desirable period depends on the nature of the work. Too frequent breaks can be irritating to staff who have to interrupt tasks in mid-stream. Too few rests can cause a loss of efficiency and increase in errors.

Control over your own fate

Everyone likes to feel that they have some control over their own lives. Systems that are flexible and adaptable give the user an opportunity to exert some influence over them.

With physical equipment, like chairs and screens, staff often fiddle around with the controls at first, then leave the equipment fixed for a long time. The important psychological point, however, is that they know they can change it, if they want to. Of course, careful monitoring of how systems are used should make sure that adjustable systems are not played about with too much or left in uncomfortable positions for other users who do not know how to tweak the controls.

At more significant levels of job roles and work routines, people are given a sense of purpose, of pride and motivation if they feel their individuality is respected within the overall corporate context.

Managers are often primarily concerned with the 'pay off' and the 'bottom line' – what a system delivers in terms of efficiency, productivity, better service or other corporate goals. Individuals are more worried about the fulfilment and rewards of their jobs.

The shape of future office jobs is unpredictable. Many different patterns will emerge, depending on how the balance is struck between what is good for the organisation and what is desirable for the individual.

6 A glimpse into the future

Towards the Outer Limits

The electronic office systems described so far in this book will be a familiar part of office life into the twenty-first century.

Of course, there will be advances and improvements. Processors will become faster, cheaper and more able to deal with a lot of tasks at the same time (*parallel processing*). Storage and memory will pack more bits into smaller spaces for less money. Optical storage, like video disks, will become more economical and will have better software assistance. Three-dimensional storage using *holograms* will become feasible.

Computer-based systems will have better eyes and ears. Voice and handwriting input will become more flexible, with the computer understanding the way people normally speak and write. Computers will be able to 'see' pictures, faces, and other images. Screens will become flatter and both smaller and larger.

Software will become more 'intelligent'. More expert systems will appear which resemble the understanding and thought-processes of human experts. *Artificial intelligence* will make software more adaptable, more able to cope with the ambiguity and fuzziness with which people usually express themselves.

In 1979, the Japanese government set a blueprint for computing developments in the 1990s, called the *Fifth Generation Computer System* (see Chapter 8 for a description of previous generations). The Fifth Generation identifies three main priorities. Firstly, computers should become easier to use by everybody. Secondly, software development should be more reliable and efficient. Finally, hardware must give better performance and a wider range of functions.

The Fifth Generation pins a lot of hope on putting more artificial intelligence into the system. Instead of having databases stuffed with facts, the Fifth Generation aims to create *Intelligent Knowledge-Based Systems (IKBS)* which contain the distilled wisdom of people. Software being developed to handle knowledge bases acts in similar ways to human logic and reasoning, deducing or inferring something on the basis of previous information and experiences. *Logic programming* languages, such as Prolog and Lisp, are the main Fifth Generation software tools.

Some of the Fifth Generation objectives of improving user/ system interactions can be achieved by human factors engineering techniques. A degree of commonsense intelligence by systems designers can also enhance the usability of computers.

The Fifth Generation expects some major new technological advances. For users, they essentially mean better value-for-money, more natural, more flexible, more varied versions of the main trends already in the electronic pipeline. Beyond the Fifth Generation, we are into the realms of science-fiction where the human imagination is the only limit (or human stupidity, if nuclear war, in which electronics would play a key part, casts its mushroom cloud over the future).

Time-warped into Dataland

As a taster of what a futuristic office might be like, deep in the heart of the twenty-first century, we could take a trip to Dataland. This is the name of a project started in the 1970s at the Massachusetts Institute of Technology (MIT), with funding from the US Department of Defence.

Dataland has been described as 'the first travel machine of the information age.' In it, you travel through 'data space'. You sit in a chair and navigate your way around the sights and sounds, the information and the digits in this data space.

At your Dataland command chair you have a variety of input control devices, such as a *cat*, a *joystick* and a remote-controlled pointer. The cat is a pad that sends signals to the screen when you touch it (*touch sensitive*). A joystick is like a gear lever that you can use to control the direction of a pointer or an object under computer control. Another device can also be used as an electronic 'paintbrush' to draw colours, shapes and lines on the wall screen by remote control.

On each side of the chair is a VDU screen. They have touch-sensitive screens that enable you to input to the system by putting your finger on the appropriate spot on the screen.

The screen on your right contains a permanent map of Dataland. It has ikons to represent particular functions (say, a calculator), and complete areas with lots of symbols (such as an office area with telephone, filing cabinet, etc). The cursor is a 'window' onto this Dataland map.

Using the joystick to move the window over the calculator ikon, you get an image of a calculator on the left hand screen. You can then touch the 'keys' of the calculator on the screen, which responds as if it were real. The Dataland 'calculator' is known as a *virtual* object because it acts as if it were a real object for all practical purposes but has no physical existence as such.

You then move the window onto the office area. The whole office 'map' with all its ikons is then enlarged to fill the right hand screen. As you move the window towards the telephone ikon you hear a low ringing. As you get closer, the virtual phone rings louder and louder in full sterophonic sound. The virtual phone appears on the left-hand screen. You 'dial' a number by touching the phone 'keys' to get through to a computer information service. You want to look through a virtual reference book. The first page appears on the screen. By stroking the electronic cat, you 'turn' the pages of the book. When you do so, the page is animated to move as it would if it were a real book.

You then data-travel to a cocktail party.

I spy with my electronic eye

On the wall-screen in front of you are live pictures of a cocktail party being held in a room wired for surveillance. With the joystick, you control a secret camera in the party room, directing it at peoples' faces. Dataland compares these faces with digitised photographs in its files.

When it recognises a face, it provides the picture on the left hand screen for your verification. If you agree, you then get a whole fact-file on the person's background.

When you have got all the low down you need on the people at the cocktail party, you navigate yourself onto a guided tour of Boston, as you will be going there soon on a real trip. You start with a satellite picture of the US. Then you zoom down through a map of Massachusetts to a map of Boston.

You are then shown a slide show of pictures of Boston. The information-space is kept up-to-date, so you can find out what is on at the cinemas or see the menus at restaurants. As you travel through virtual Boston, the stereophonic sound gives you a feel of what it will be like in the real Boston.

Most of the facilities of Dataland described here were working at MIT in 1980, although some were in very crude experimental forms. Electronic information technology can give birth to the inconceivable.

Moving the office into the home

Predicting the impact of information technology beyond that already attempted earlier in the book is best left to poets and science fiction writers. What happens in office work will depend on what happens in society at large – and there are so many factors at play that futorology cannot be regarded as an exact science.

For example, it is often forecast that the electronic office will lead to more work being done from home. If this does happen on any major scale, it would have tremendous implications for family life, marriage, community facilities, education and property development. It is extremely difficult to see the outcome of such social change, even at a time of relative technological calm.

The managing director in Chapter 2 illustrates the most glamorous way in which home-based office work is likely to occur. She lives in a spacious home, with room for her office. She has a choice about when to work at home and when to go into an office.

The traditional nature of home-based work has been very different. It has often been poorly paid, high pressure work. The picture of an 'office in the home' is less attractive if the home is cramped, the worker is poor and the work is grindingly monotonous, say 'power typing' on a word processor.

The social circumstances of the home worker, the level of unemployment in the community, the kinds of local services available (like crêches and nursery schools), the way home workers are paid – these are the crucial factors, not the availability of particular electronic wizardry.

Comes the revolution. . . .

In the long-term, the 'information revolution' is likely to cause more changes in society than previous agricultural and industrial revolutions. It is taking place in so many ways, in so many places, at a time when society is already going through volatile economic, social and political developments.

The same software-controlled digital techniques of the electronic office are also being used to shed new light on other sciences and technologies, from genetic engineering to weather forecasting. Cruise missiles are controlled by software and chips. Life-saving medical research and equipment depend on computers. Children learn and play with computers.

Technological optimists point to previous periods of technological change to show that they ultimately led to more jobs and improved material well-being. Pessimists point to the trauma caused over many years during the transition, the frictions and schisms that still reverberate throughout society, and the negative effects of some technologies, such as pollution of the atmosphere.

Information technology can boost and consolidate the power of individuals and groups who are already in positions of influence. It can heap benefits on the 'haves' and take away the last vestiges of dignity and self-determination from the 'have-nots'.

Information technology can also be the means of creating an informed democracy, responsive at the grassroots, sensitive and effective in central planning. It can give sight to the blind, hearing to the deaf, strength to the underdeveloped, a more satisfying life to everyone, at work, rest and play.

Comes the information revolution. . . .? We will have to wait and see the history of the future before there is an answer.

End of the body, start of the pool

This is the end of the body of the book. The next three chapters are a pool into which you can dip occasionally.

7   Your quick-check advisor

Top twenty questions

This book has covered a lot of electronic office territory. It has told you about the vast variety of technological aids that are available, how they can affect your lives, and what you may be able to do about it.

Chapters 4 and 5 summarise a great deal of advice from the experiences of many users. This chapter further distils that guidance into answers to twenty key questions. These should be read in conjunction with the relevant sections in Chapters 4 and 5 which explore the issues in more depth. The 'I' in the questions below could be an individual or group, covering a lot of different jobs, backgrounds, organisations and companies. Each office requires its own unique solutions.

Your quick-check advisor cannot provide you with a recipe for success every time. It can, however, try to point you in the right directions; warn you of the dangers ahead; and wish you well in your exploration and examination of the electronic office.

Am I missing out if I am not using the latest electronic office equipment now?
Possibly, but not necessarily. In the long run, most office work will be aided by some form of electronic information system. New office technology, however, is no panacea. Poorly designed and implemented systems can replace a muddled, inefficient but workable manual office system with an inefficient automated mess.

Evo-revolution is the watchword. Do not rush into the electronic office just because you feel you are 'being left behind' or that it will solve all your problems. Look carefully at what you are doing now, what the technology offers, and then act, starting gently on a well-planned route.

Taking it slowly at first must not be an excuse for inaction. If you have thoroughly explored your requirements and feel you need some new office technology, don't delay. At the very least, start to find out more about what the electronic office could do for (and to) you.

How can new office systems assist me?
In the many ways described in this book – and more. To decide what they can (and cannot) do in your particular circumstances, there is no alternative to a systematic and careful study. This should take the following course.
● Think about the long term. Prepare a planned strategy.
● Look at what you are doing now; what skills are needed to carry out today's jobs.
● Identify what you like and dislike about the current set up. What is being done well, what is being done inefficiently.
● Find out as much as you can about the functions that can be performed by new office technology.
● Explore in more depth the aids that seem most likely to be of assistance to you.
● Examine how to improve the current situation in ways that do not use new technology. Changes in office procedures, staff motivation and training can often be a tonic in themselves.
● Try out the most promising new systems. Seek professional and technical advice on alternative approaches.
● Start using new technology in a planned, step-by-step way.
● As you gain more experience, adapt your strategy. Proceed more quickly when your confidence grows.

Where do I get advice?
General advice can be obtained in books such as this one; in TV programmes, such as the BBC Computer Literacy series; on videos and in magazines and newspapers. More specific advice relating to your own circumstances should come from trade associations and trade unions, specialists within your organisation (if there are any), or from independent consultants who should understand your line of activity as well as the technology.

The best advice is likely to come from people in the same boat as yourself. Seek out others who have used similar systems. Contact any user groups for the systems that most interest you or who cover similar types of applications to your own. In some activities there are national and industry-wide guidelines and standards for information systems. Within organisations, there are also likely to be corporate information, computing and personnel policies that can be followed.

What type and size of system should I be looking for?

There are so many reasonably-priced options now available that you could find a huge number of different types of system, with a variety of marketing labels to meet your needs. You therefore need to narrow your search without missing out on some important possibilities. Here are a few hints about your first sift through the market place.

- Make a list of your current activities and your likely future ones.
- Assign priorities to tasks in the list – which are most important, which are least.
- Take the most vital tasks as the 'core' of what you are looking for.
- Work out how much you have got to spend (see question about costs below).
- Quantify the volume of information you deal with (eg number of clients' records, average number of words in each record, etc).
- Identify and quantify the *transactions* that take place in the office, such as number of queries answered; time expected to answer a query; number of times a file is updated; and so on.
- How many workstations are likely to be needed? Too few can cause staff frustration and under-use of the system. Too many is wasteful.
- How many workstations may need to be online to the system at any one time?
- Is a stand-alone system acceptable?
- Do the software, files and communications have to be compatible with other systems?
- How reliable should it be? Must the system be available over 99% of the time or can I get by with something less?
- For each of the factors above, what are the immediate and foreseeable needs? What are the long-term requirements?

What are the likely benefits of the electronic office?

You need to consider the following questions to determine what the likely benefits may be, remembering qualitative are as important as quantified advantages.

- Where can new technology add value?
- What new services to customers and clients can it provide?
- How can it improve existing services?
- How can jobs be made more satisfying and effective?
- How can the working environment be improved?
- How can productivity be increased?

- How can technology reduce existing costs?
- How can the overall running of the organisation be made more effective and efficient?
- How can the flow of information within the organisation be improved?
- What aids can be provided to assist decision making?

What are the possible costs involved?

There are more factors (some qualitative, some quantifiable) that contribute to the cost of a system than the most obvious direct ones. You should examine the following.

- The price of *all* hardware and software (including storage and input/output peripherals).
- Ancilliaries and accessories – ribbons, new stationery, storage for tapes and disks, cables, power supplies, noise dampers (*acoustic hoods*) for printers, etc.
- Training for *all* staff, not just operators.
- Support from suppliers, both for routine maintenance and to ensure a quick and reliable response to breakdowns.
- Changes to the building and environment (see question on office buildings below).
- Cost of consultants, books, magazines and other forms of obtaining advice.
- Transferring information from manual records to computerised form.
- The transition period, when software and existing computer data files may have to be converted to the new system and the old manual methods may be run in parallel with the new system for a time.
- The organisational cost if social and human factors are badly handled (managerial and staff resistance, disruption of established working methods, over-formalisation and structuring of procedures, and so on).
- The personal cost if jobs become more monotonous, stressful, deskilled, isolated.
- Insurance both of equipment and against 'consequential loss' if there is a serious failure.
- Installation. Some manufacturers include delivery to the door in their price but not moving systems into the office and getting them running.
- Cost of hesitation. What benefits are lost if there is too long a delay in getting a system?
- Cost of failure. What happens to the organisation and to

individuals when there are system failures? What is the impact on customers and clients?

What will happen to my job?

Whatever your office job is, or whatever office job you want to do, it will change at some time in the future because of new office technology.

There will be a reduction, in the short-term at least, in certain jobs. Some jobs will be automated out of existence. New jobs will be created and, in the long-term, some existing jobs will expand. All jobs will require new skills. Some will have more challenging skills than now, others will be de-skilled.

For those in work, the following are important factors affecting the nature of the job.
● Pre-programming and computer-control. The degree to which the job is determined by the software and the leeway given to individuals to use their initiative.
● Alienation and isolation from other staff.
● Variety of skills needed to do a job.
● Freedom to make your own decisions about where, when and how to work.
● Salaries and special payments, perks and fringe benefits.
● Career development opportunites.
● Pressure and stress at work.
● The extent to which the computer monitors work performance.
● Whether decisions are taken mainly on the basis of rules built into a computer.
● Degree of monotony and repetition in work tasks.
● How work tasks are integrated into complete roles or fragmented into isolated activities.

What are unions doing about new office technology?

Generally, unions have welcomed technological change in office work *provided* their members share in the benefits and are protected from bad consequences. Office staff are less unionised than manual and 'blue collar' workers in manufacturing industry, although 'white collar' office unions are often strong in public services and some industries, such as banking and insurance.

Unions have put forward new technology agreements as the framework within which they would like the electronic office to be introduced. The main topics covered in technology agreements are as follows.

● Job security. Ideally, unions would like a guarantee that the number of jobs will remain the same. In most cases they accept agreements that there will be no compulsory redundancy; that adequate payment for voluntary redundancies will be made; early retirement offered; and natural wastage (not replacing staff who leave) permitted.

● Consultation. Unions would like to receive full information, in plain language before any change takes place. They may ask for participation in systems design by trained technology representatives, and access to their own independent consultants.

● *Status quo.* Unions would like no change to take place until agreement has been reached between management and unions.

● Training and redeployment. Adequate training in skills for the electronic office is sought. Unions would like staff with skills and jobs no longer required to be retrained and given priority when vacancies arise in jobs with new skills and opportunities.

● Performance monitoring. Unions are wary of computers being used to monitor and pace work.

● Hours and conditions. Unions want technology to help reduce working hours and improve pay and the general work environment. They are against staff losing status or pay when moving to new jobs.

● Health and safety. Unions are concerned that adequate standards are adhered to (see question on health and safety of VDUs below).

● Job design. Unions wish to avoid 'Taylorisation' of office jobs and want to have a say in how jobs are designed.

What kind of training is needed and how can I get it?
Most people will need to learn a new skill to use and understand electronic office systems. The general education and training system should provide adequate background and some specific skills because using information technology is as important to coping with the modern world as reading, writing and mathematics.

One of the criteria used when selecting a system should be how it helps with training, such as its ease of operation, Computer Assisted Learning software, HELP facilities, plain-language and effective documentation, training courses from the supplier, etc. Employers should also provide sufficient training and retraining.

The following are some new key skills needed.

- Operating particular equipment. Understanding the full potential of the system.
- Understanding the *principles* of software-controlled information processing.
- Understanding how information files can be organised on computer systems.
- Learning how to search through computerised databases and the types of query languages used.
- How to decide if a system has good human factors engineering.
- Ability to interpret systems design specifications and to undertake your own analysis and design of systems.
- How to make best use of electronic mail communications.
- Maximising the benefits of decision support systems.
- Being able to exploit fully the flexibility and power of word processors (applies to managers and professionals, as well as secretaries and typists).
- Performing jobs in conjunction with a computer-based system rather than on your own.
- What to do if somthing goes wrong with your system.
- How to challenge technological 'experts'.

Do I need to learn how to program a computer?
Only if your job is going to involve developing software or you have the desire to write your own software. In order to use a computer-based system, however, you do not need to know how to program, just as you do not need to be a telephone engineer to use the telephone or a motor mechanic to drive a car.

Understanding the basic principles and concepts of digital information systems is of value. So is getting a 'feel' of what programming is like by writing some very simple programs in a language like Basic, designed for beginners.

You should avoid trying to develop your own software for work unless you have a strong aptitude for programming. Writing programs for fun on a home computer is a different kettle of bugs to producing 'serious' software for use at work. If you attempt to write your own programs for the office, you could find that you waste a lot of time and money and still end up with an unreliable, possibly unusable tangle of programming spaghetti.

How easy are electronic office systems to use?
It all depends on how seriously and systematically the supplier

has followed good ergonomics and human factors practice. Here are a few guidelines on what to look for to see how 'user friendly' a system is.

- The language of the dialogue between the user and the system, including error messages, should be understandable and unambiguous.
- Starting, running and ending tasks should be easy and should fit the user's natural way of thinking about and carrying out a task.
- The system should be 'user profilable', flexible and adaptable.
- Beginners and more experienced users may need different user/system interactions.
- An error in one part or module should not bring the whole system crashing down.
- Commands, codes, labels on keys, etc should be easy to remember and have a clear relation to the task or function they perform.
- When you do something 'silly', like inputting '31 February' as a date or keying in that one hundred items of a product that never sells more than ten at a time have been ordered, the system should query your input. Mistakes in data entry are a major source of error in computer systems.
- The system should be polite and not use interjections like 'Eh?'
- Appropriate methods of searching through databases should be provided.
- You should be asked for confirmation of any irretrievable act, like erasing a file.
- You should never be left up in the air, not knowing what to do next.
- When there is a fault, the system should clearly state what may be wrong, what corrective action you can take (if any), and what your next step should be.
- There should be consistency in the codes and language you use when moving between tasks or from beginner to experienced levels.
- Easy ways of turning numerical information into graphs should be provided.
- CAL and HELP facilities should be built into the software.
- The system should be available when you need it and not break down often.
- What is shown on a word processor screen should be similar to its hard copy output.

- Documentation provided with the system should be clear and efficient to use.
- Response times should be appropriate to the task being undertaken.
- If the system fails while typing a long report, you should not have to start again.
- Hardware should be designed to good ergonomic standards (see next question).

Are VDUs and word processors a danger to health?
There is no confirmed evidence that screen-based systems emit an excessive amount of radiation or pose any other direct health hazard. But badly designed equipment in a poor work environment can lead to physical discomfort and pyschological pressure.

The answer given above to the question 'What will happen to my job?' suggests how job design can help to alleviate and avoid psychological problems. The 'ease of use' criteria in the previous question can also make jobs more pleasant. The following are some important factors that mainly relate to physical aspects. (See also pages 112 to 118 which look in more detail at ergonomic issues.)
- Screen and keyboard should be separated.
- There should be adequate work space on desks.
- Characters on the screen should be clear and steady. Brightness should be adjustable.
- The screen should be tiltable and rotatable.
- Character and background colours should be acceptable for prolonged operation.
- Lighting should be adequate. There should be no glare from the screen.
- The keyboard should be slim with properly shaped, non-glossy surfaces.
- Labels on keys should be understandable.
- Special function keys should be indentified by special colours and positioning.
- When a key for an important action is pressed, an audible signal should be given to re-assure the operator.
- Noise levels where printers are used should be kept within acceptable limits.
- Chairs should be on castors. Height, back and neck rests should be adjustable.
- Desks should not be too low or too high.
- Regular eye tests and appropriate spectacles should be pro-

vided for operators.

● Regular rest periods should be taken by operators, particularly those doing monotonous work.

● Temperature, humidity, the amount of electric static in a room, and other environmental factors should be controlled and monitored.

● Document holders should be used where appropriate.

● Regular checks should be made to see that standards are maintained.

What if a new system is landed on my desk one morning without warning?

Many people, at all except the top levels of organisations, have found themselves in this position. Systems have been introduced without prior consultation or provision of information. The response from staff has sometimes been to go on strike, refuse to work with new technology, or to take some other direct action.

In many cases, there has been a reluctant acceptance, with less obvious resistance. Managers and staff avoid learning how to use the system, often subconsciously, Resentment and irritation builds up. Mistakes are made. There is indifference and apathy to the new systems and a failure to exploit their full potential.

If you are faced with a system imposed on you without consultation, what you can do about it will depend on your position in the organisation, how managers deal with complaints, the strength of the union or staff association, and other circumstances. The following are some positive steps you can take.

● Make a case explaining why the system would have been more effective if you and your colleagues had been involved at an earlier stage.

• Point out that systems tend to be more appropriate to real working needs if the people who are most affected by them have a say in how they are chosen and implemented.

• Explain that the fear and resentment generated by not being forewarned could lead to various forms of inefficiencies and resistance.

• Do not feel intimidated by the technology.

• Try to examine your system objectively. Use guidelines in this book, and other sources of information, to be specific about what you like and dislike about the system (ease of use, physical ergonomics, work practices imposed to accommodate the system, job design, etc).

• Find out what is feasible to do to improve the systems, short of completely rejecting it. Considerable improvement can sometimes be made with different software, or different work methods and organisational procedures involving the system.

• By a critically constructive approach, try to ensure that when the system is updated or replaced, you are involved in the selection and design of the new system.

• See how a technology agreement could provide a framework that would avoid this happening in the future.

If I have the choice, how do I ensure I get the right system?
Computer-based systems are powerful and complex. There is no way to guarantee you will avoid mistakes. Until you gain experience you should be as careful as possible and take the following precautionary measures.

• Regard learning-by-experience as important. Encourage an open atmosphere where difficulties can be discussed and overcome so the system will continually be improved.

• Adopt a planned, step-by-step approach to problems, which can be sorted out before moving to the next step.

• Follow the advice given in Chapters 4 and 5 and the summaries given in this chapter on deciding what you want, organisation and job design, staff relations, training, and characteristics of 'user friendly' ergonomic design.

• Talk to other users of similar systems.

• To ensure that systems meet your real working requirements those who will operate them or be directly affected by them should have an opportunity to comment on alternatives before a choice is made.

● If possible, get some hands-on experience of the system, preferably in your own working environment. At least use the system at the supplier's demonstration centre.
● Take care in selecting a supplier (see answer to next question).

Are suppliers of systems trustworthy?
As in most highly competitive businesses, some are trustworthy and some are not. The volatility of the market place has meant that the industry is in a continuous state of flux – new companies come and go; older ones keeping changing, adding new products, dropping others; companies merge and join in co-operative ventures.

Chapter 8 describes the background to the companies supplying electronic office products and services. The following are some important questions suppliers should be asked. Their answers will indicate whether you are dealing with a respectable company or a fly-by-night operation.
● How long has the company been in business?
● How many staff are employed? What do they do? Where are they located?
● What is the company's financial record? What financial backing does it have?
● How long has the system(s) you are interested in been available? How many users are there? What applications is it used for?
● What is the total number of the company's computer-based systems currently installed by users?
● What are the numbers and locations of service centres?
● Are there any user groups associated with the supplier and/or particular systems? Can you have the names and addresses of users who you can contact?

What office tasks should be tackled first by electronic systems?
This will depend, of course, on the kind of work being done but these are some general guidelines.
● The initial applications should fit into a longer-term, step-by-step strategy.
● Pilot projects should be considered to gain experience without affecting the main flow of the organisation's work.
● Initial applications should not be trivial ones but they should also not be so central to an organisation's activities that teething problems have major and highly visible effects within the organisation and for clients and customers.
● Experience gained in the initial steps should be carefully

analysed and lessons learnt for future, larger steps.

● 'Log books' should be kept, possibly in the form of videos of users reactions before and after installation. These can help in analysing the experience and also act as a means of informing others of what the experience has been like.

● Employees not involved in the initial systems should be kept informed of what is happening to avoid rumours spreading and to explain why changes in procedures may take place.

● Customers, clients, and other people your organisation deals with reguarly should be kept informed of changes and how they should improve your relations with them.

● If the initial applications fail, be prepared to start afresh if you can. Sometimes, trying to battle on with a poor system can be more trouble and expense than cutting short your losses and using your experience to build on a firmer foundation.

What kind of typing is most suited to word processing?
If your typing work consists mainly of one-off letters and memos, an electronic typewriter can provide almost as much productivity improvement as a more powerful and expensive word processor. Screen-based word processors are of maximum benefit with the following kinds of typing.

● Longish reports that go through many draft revisions.

● Letters with standard text but a few changes to each, such as names and addresses, as needed for mail shots.

● Legal documents, contracts, and other documents made up from standard clauses, paragraphs, etc.

● Documents that have to be produced to a tight deadline and where it is important to have good presentation of the final version.

● Work with a lot of complex layout requirements, tables, scientific formulae, and so on.

Can new technology fit into existing office buildings?
Usually it can but sometimes only after considerable alteration. New buildings should be constructed taking into account the cabling, air conditioning and other environmental needs of electronic office equipment. Although staff numbers in some office jobs may decline, some extra space is sometimes needed for equipment, so the total need for office space may not decline, at least in the short-term.

The following are some considerations that might affect buildings and interior decoration.

• Special cabling is usually needed. Coaxial cables can be much fatter than traditional telephone wiring. This could mean alterations to provide sufficient cabling ducts in the right places. Cabling needs to be concealed if possible, so false floors and ceilings, pillars, etc, may be needed.

• Air conditioning must be of the right standard, which could lead to having new boilers, cooling towers, ducts and other equipment.

• There should be sufficient electrical outlets to allow flexibility in positioning equipment.

• Lighting needs to be adequate in all parts of the working environment.

• Space may be wanted for storing magnetic tapes and disks.

• Curtains, blinds, carpets, and wall decorations may be changed for ergonomic reasons.

• Extra physical security procedures may need to be installed because of the importance of electronic systems and the sensitivity of the information held on them. This could mean special locks and access mechanisms on doors, strengthening of windows, and so on.

• Sound proofing may be needed in rooms with noisy printers.

Will computers be used to invade my personal privacy?
It all depends on what safeguards are taken against misuse of computerised information and the behaviour of people who are allowed to look at files containing information about you. Information has always been vulnerable to prying eyes, even in traditional manual files. Computers add a new dimension to the dangers.

One of the main aims of computerised databases is to allow the same information to be accessed quickly, from many locations, for a variety of different tasks. Software techniques can be used to prevent access to certain files. Information can also be encrypted to make it difficult to decode, particularly when it is being sent by telecommunications. Physical security can also be used to prevent unwarranted access to terminals and files.

In the end, however, people with rightful access to information may be corrupt, malicious or carrying out the orders of a government or company that aims to persecute particular individuals or groups. Data protection legislation has been passed in many countries to discourage such abuses.

Laws vary between countries in their scope (the type of files excluded), the means of licensing or registering databases, who investigates complaints, and what happens when offences have been committed. These are some principles:

● Information collected about you for one purpose should not be used for another without your consent (this protects, for example, medical records being looked at by anyone other than medical professionals).

● You have the right to check information about yourself and change anything incorrect.

● Some information can be kept only for a set period of time.

● Organisations holding databases need to have some form of licence or registration.

● You can take action against any organisation misusing information and breaking data protection laws.

● Information cannot be transferred to countries that do not have their own data protection laws.

What can I do if something goes wrong with my system?
It all depends on the preparations and precautions you have taken beforehand. If you follow the advice in this book, you should be less likely to encounter really serious problems – and if you do, you should be well protected.

Summarising earlier advice:

● Have a long-term strategy split into evolutionary steps to limit damage should problems occur at earlier stages.

● Be cautious about the initial applications.

● Take care when choosing systems and suppliers.

● Make sure you have adequate support, maintenance and repair arrangements, even if they are a significant expense.

● Have adequate back-up for hardware, storage and for the system as a whole.

● Give priority to hardware and software that have inbuilt aids for detecting and correcting errors.

● Take out insurance on the hardware. Also cover 'consequential loss' to the organisation if information is lost or the system is not operational for a substantial period.

● Be sure that the contract(s) with the supplier(s) clearly, and in detail, defines the performance you expect, who is responsible for aspects of the system's operation and what action can be taken if any party fails to live up to the contract.

● Check on how consumer protection, data protection, health and safety, and other legislation applies to your circumstances.

● Contact technical, local or national press, radio or TV. Write to the supplier's public relations department.

8 Roots of the electronic office

So, what's new?

There are some neophiles (lovers of the new) who seem to believe that the world began the day their latest technological fad was invented. The development of science and technology, however, is a continuous process of learning, experimenting, experiencing and re-learning.

The roots of the electronic office lie in many different technical, scientific and industrial soils. These have combined into the main thrust of digital computer-based information technology, which has branched out into a kaleidoscope of uses.

The body of this book has presented many of the items that have blossomed on the electronic office branch of information technology. This chapter delves back into the roots. As commercial and technological developments have been so closely intertwined, it starts with a look at the way the information technology industry has grown.

A quick tour of the market place

Understanding the marketing practices of suppliers is as important as knowing about the technology when you are looking to obtain a system.

The modern computing industry emerged in the early 1960s. The *mainframe* computers available then were so large and expensive they could be afforded only by big companies and public organisations (the term 'mainframe' comes from the large structure used to house the processor and main memory). There were no online terminals originally. Input had to be sent physically to the computer centre, where it was put into batches for processing (this was rather obviously called *batch* processing).

Mainframe manufacturers tended to provide all the hardware and software in a wrapped up bundle. They also provided their users with a lot of advice, training, special software and other support. In the late 1960s, when all things trendy were mini, a new kind of computer made an impact, the *minicomputer*.

These were smaller, cheaper and more rugged than mainframes and were first used in industrial tasks, like controlling chemical manufacturing processes. Minis did not need the molly-coddling of mainframes, which were housed in huge rooms with special temperature, humidity and dust controls.

Mini manufacturers were mainly concerned with 'shifting iron' – selling the hardware as cheaply as possible. Minis came with basic software tools that could be used to build programs to carry out the tasks required by the user.

The mainframers sold directly to their customers. Mini vendors often sold via *third party* dealers and *systems houses*. A *systems house* takes in other manufacturers' equipment, adds their own software and then packages the total system for customers, sometimes even putting their own label on the hardware.

The systems house is an example of an *OEM*, a company which creates a system or device that includes components or a complete computer from another company. Nobody seems sure whether the initials OEM stand for Original Equipment Manufacturer or Other Equipment Manufacturer.

Software in the ascendency

Mainframers, systems houses and specialist companies picked up the challenge of the mini by developing *small business systems*. These have the power of the mini, the packaging and support of a mainframe and are priced between a stripped-down mini and the smaller mainframes. Despite some environmental problems, like heat generation, small business systems need less pampering than a mainframe and can run in a normal office.

As hardware began to spread, it became clear that the supply of good software was insufficient to meet user demand. Software development proved to be error-prone, costly, unreliable and unpredictable. *Software houses* were established solely to create and develop software.

Mainframe manufacturers also began to *unbundle* the cost of software from the hardware because they realised that software was a major slice of their costs. Mini manufacturers gave more priority to software and started to be more like mainframers in their approach to supporting customers.

Batch processing proved to be an expensive bottleneck for most tasks. Online terminals, small business systems and minis brought computing power closer to where the user action was.

The computing scene was already a buzz of activity when the

micro hit the market in the 1970s, with the impact of a Molotov cocktail.

All shook up by the micro

Micros made minis and mainframes cheaper, smaller and more powerful. They also created a new microcomputer industry. ('Micro' is used as an abbreviation for either a *micro* chip with a processor or memory on it, or a complete *micro*computer that includes a processor, memory, input, output and communications links, usually on more than one chip.)

Micro chips can expand minis into *maxis* and *superminis* with a performance and range of capabilities overlapping that of mainframes. Micros also bloated mainframes into giant, high speed *supercomputers*. At their lower end, mainframes came down in price and size, meeting minis going up.

Before micros, terminals were generally *dumb* – they relied for their processing and memory on central computers. *Intelligent terminals* emerged that could stand alone with their own clever chips inside them or join up with other workstations in a communications network.

Microcomputers sell in quantities undreamed of by early mainframe and mini vendors. This mass market creates opportunities for software suppliers to sell vast numbers of products. *Software publishers* have sprung up who package and market programs written by independent 'authors', hoping for a 'best seller', just as book publishers do.

The pace of progress triggered by the micro has been fabulous. If motor car developments had matched those in micros, a Rolls Royce would now cost about 50 cents, do 3000 miles to the gallon – and you could put 50 of them through the eye of a needle!

Where the sharks lurk

A mainframe has a relatively high price. The supplier therefore does not have to sell too many to make sufficient profit to provide users with a considerable amount of training and support. Many more minis have to be sold to make a similar profit, particularly as mainframes are usually sold direct to customers, whereas minis have a third party systems house or dealer to take a rake off.

Mini vendors generally provide less support than do mainframe manufacturers. Microcomputer prices have to be kept extremely low in a competitive, even cut-throat business. So they really have to sell like fastfood burgers to make a profit.

Microcomputer dealers and manufacturers therefore often cut profit margins to the bone in order to 'shift iron' and keep the cash flowing in. The result is that support to the customer is sometimes also squeezed to the minimum and users can be left high and dry if something goes wrong.

Software development generally costs around the same amount whether it is for a mainframe, mini or microcomputer. The price structure for software products, however, is similar to that of hardware, with micro software costing a fraction of the price that would be paid for the equivalent product on a mainframe. Unless their product is sufficiently popular to give them enough revenue to offer adequate support, software suppliers may provide some pretty threadbare after-sales service.

This does not mean that you are necessarily safer with a mainframe or mini supplier than with microcomputer companies. You should be careful to check out just what you are getting from any supplier, as recommended earlier in this book. There are some excellent hardware and software products and suppliers in all parts of the market. There are also many sharks lurking in the lucrative electronic office waters.

Horses for courses

The nature of particular systems often reflects the origins of their pioneers. Take, for example, the difference between word processing on a dedicated word processor and a microcomputer.

Word processors were developed primarily by companies in the office equipment business. The keyboard, screen and software were designed to carry out editing and other word processing functions as their top priority. Many of them have only word processing software.

Microcomputers, on the other hand, were first created as cheap and cheerful computers for enthusiasts at home. Later, more business-like systems were marketed with a similar range of 'Jack-of-all-trades, master of many' software packages to their mainframe and mini ancestors.

Software for word processing on a microcomputer is likely to be inferior to a dedicated word processor in its ease of use and range of facilities, although perfectly adequate for the needs of many owners of microcomputers.

An example of the difference between word processing on a micro and a purpose-built machine is the way the cursor on the screen is controlled. A word processor usually has special cursor-control keys with an arrow on each to indicate whether that key moves the cursor up, down, left or right. On a micro, you may have to press two keys to move the cursor, say a CONTROL key and the letter 'J' to move left and CONTROL and 'K' to move right.

Some upmarket business microcomputers and larger computer systems can provide high quality word processing. But whereas a cheap microcomputer costs less than a word processor, once you move into the more professional micro market, that price difference vanishes.

It really is a matter of 'horses for courses' when selecting a system, which is why it is wise to go through the procedures discussed in Chapter 4.

Where word processors come from

Word processors that could be recognised as such by today's standards first appeared in the early 1960s. The history of techniques for handling words goes back much further.

Movable type was used in China in the eleventh century and in Europe in the fifteenth century, thanks to innovators like Johann Gutenberg in Germany and William Caxton in England. A form of mechanical typing was patented in 1714 in England but it was not until 1867 that the first typewriter was built by Sholes, Glidden and Soulé in Milwaukee, USA. Seven years later, typewriters went into commercial production by E. Remington and Sons, under contract to the original trio.

In the next 100 years, changes occurred gradually. For example, in 1902, an electric typewriter with a single-element print mechanism was introduced, called the Blickendorfer. About 60 years later, IBM brought out the Selectric with its single-element golfball printing method.

The first automatic typewriter was developed in the 1920s by an American company, Shultz, who also made perforated paper rolls for pianolas. Holes positioned in these rolls operated the keys to play the music on the pianola. Shultz applied this concept of punched paper input to control typewriters automatically in the relatively popular 'Auto-Typist', which was manufactured under licence by the Automatic Typewriter Company.

The idea of editing text was given concrete form during the Second World War when the US army commissioned IBM to make an automatic typewriter to write personalised letters to next-of-kin war casualties. This allowed sections of the standard text to be omitted and new sections to be inserted.

Typewriters smarten up

In 1964, IBM, which is also the world's largest computer manufacturer, made another important typewriter innovation. It introduced the Selectric Magnetic Tape Typewriter, which gave the typewriter the ability to store prepared text on magnetically-coated devices, such as magnetic tape and magnetic cards, rather than on the clumsier, slower and less capacious paper tape.

Typewriters with two memories later appeared from a number of suppliers. Input could come from one memory, the text edited from the keyboard and then output to the second memory. Such *memory typewriters* were the direct predecessors of today's electronic typewriters.

Screen-based word processors with much larger processing and storage capabilities derived from merging developments in computing with the work evolving from typewriters. The VDU is really the prototype of the screen word processor. It was originally developed for use as a terminal linked to mainframes and minis.

In the 1970s, many *text processing* software packages were developed for minis and mainframes that did the editing tasks now expected of word processors. The term 'word processing' was first introduced in the early 1960s by IBM, as a translation of the term 'Textverarbeitung'. This was coined by an IBM salesman, Herr Stilhilper, to describe a mixed dictation and typing system. 'Word processing' is a label still sometimes applied to dictation systems but its accepted meaning is for the computer-based systems described in this book.

Of course, as the micro chip shrank the size of processors and main memory, minis and mainframes were no longer needed to provide the computing power for word processing. Computing and microelectronics had joined up to transform the office equipment industry, just one of the many branches of information technology.

Back to the abacus – and beyond

Computing is a central theme in the electronic office and all information technology. Its roots go back deep into pre-history. Stonehenge and other similar pre-historic constructions were primative aids to help calculate the position of the sun and other astronomical information.

It is the abacus, however, that is the most tangible starting

point for computers. An abacus consisting of stones manipulated on a flat surface was used by the early Greeks and Romans (abacus means 'flat surface' in Latin). The Chinese and Japanese developed a much more sophisticated abacus thousands of years BC which had beads (called *calculi*) on a special frame – from which we derive the word *calculate*.

In the hands of a skilled operator, the abacus is an extremely quick form of calculator, surpassed only by the lightning speeds of electronic devices. It was not until the 17th Century that Europeans came up with anything to compete with the abacus as a calculator.

The French philospher and mathematician Blaise Pascal made an 'Arithmetic Engine' or Pascaline in 1647 to help his father, who was a judge in a tax court. The Pascaline worked in a similar way to a car milometer, with digits represented by teeth on a wheel. When one wheel goes round a complete cycle of ten teeth, it notches up one unit on the wheel next to it. In about 1667, another philospher and mathematician, the German Gottfried Leibniz, produced a calculator with more sophisticated cogs and wheels that could do multiplication and division directly, whereas the Pascaline could only do additions and subtractions.

Little happened on the calculating front for over 150 years. Then the real 'father' of modern computing, British engineer, mathematician and horse racing enthusiast Charles Babbage revealed a plan for his *Difference Engine* in 1821. This worked on a mathematical method based on calculating the difference between numbers.

Building a Difference Engine required precision engineering for accurate construction of the cogs and other components. These production problems proved too much for Babbage and he never got beyond making a small prototype.

In about 1833, Babbage abandoned his Difference Engine in favour of a more flexible machine – a *general purpose* computing device called the Analytical Engine. Although it took more than 100 years to fulfil, Babbage had laid down the blueprint for the modern computer.

The computer age gathers pace

Charles Babbage realised that his original Difference Engine had a fundamental limitation. If it were built, it could be used only for the purpose for which it was first designed and constructed. To do another task, it would have to be completely reengineered. The Analytical Engine would be *programmable* so that it could be used for many purposes.

The basic elements of the difference engine are the same as today's computer-based systems: input, store, Arithmetic Unit, Control Unit, output. The Arithmetic Unit and Control Unit comprise what is now called the *Central Processing Unit (CPU)* of a computer, or just plain *processor*.

Babbage did not have the means to give substance to his vision. Even doing the drawings for the mechanical components of his Analytical Engine proved too much for him. After Babbage computing progress went into slow motion again for another 100 years.

There were many developments in other types of calculating aids, such as tabulators, adding machines and comptometers. They were slow and limited in terms of today's computers but were efficient and effective in their day.

The next milestone was in 1935 when Konrad Zuse built the first computer based on digital binary techniques – on a table in his parent's living room in Germany. Early in the Second World War, his plan for building a more advanced version was turned down by Adolph Hitler who thought the War would end before a computer could be developed.

In Britain there was a different War story. The Polish secret service had stolen a German code generator called Enigma. A team of top mathematicians assembled at Bletchley Park then built the first electronic computer, Colossus. This played an important role during the War because it could decipher secret German messages.

In America, computers were first developed to compile ballistic tables for new guns and missiles. The most advanced of these computers became operational shortly after the War, in 1946. It was developed by John Mauchly and J. Prespert Eckert of the University of Pennsylvania and was called the Electronic Numerical Integrator and Calculator (ENIAC).

ENIAC, like Colossus, was a special-purpose electronic computer. The final step to the modern computer was still to come. Mauchly and Eckert, together with a leading mathematician, John von Neumann, produced a report in 1945 for the design of EDVAC, the Electronic Discrete Variable Automatic Computer.

EDVAC was the first full realisation of Babbage's Analytical Engine. Its *stored program control* for the first time enabled software to be input at the time it was needed. Previously, programs had to be built into the basic design of the machine.

Lady Ada and a lot of Boole

From here, computing took flight on the wings of software. EDVAC was not built until 1951. The honour of the first stored program computer in action went to the Manchester University Mark 1 in England, which ran its first program in June 1948. And in 1951, Lyons' Electronic Office, LEO, roared its message to the future.

The first-ever program was written by Charles Babbage to calculate a mathematical notion. His assistant, Lady Ada Lovelace, discovered a bug in the program and set the trend for programmers, who now spend a large part of their time *debugging* (getting rid of errors).

Mathematics has played a crucial role in computing. In particular, the nineteenth century British mathematician George Boole provided the means of creating digital computers, although he was unaware of the use to which his mathematical logic would be put.

Boolean algebra deals with the truth or falsehood of statements. *True* and *false* are the only Boolean values. This is a binary system; 'true' and 'false' could also be represented as '0' and '1'. All ordinary mathematical operations (+, −, ×, ÷) can be broken down into Boolean operations. So, deep in your word processor, workstation or microcomputer, the heart of the processor is whirring to a Boolean beat.

The Boolean operations are represented by electronic circuits in the processor. In the *first generation* computers of the 1940s and 50s, thermionic values were used as switches to control the path of electronic pulses in circuits. They were the same type of valves as used in early 'steam radio' and TV sets. Many thousand of valves were used in computers. They worked but were unreliable and clumsy. The 'main frame' of racks needed to house the valves filled huge halls.

Turning on the tranny

Shortly after the Second World War, a team under William Shockley at Bell Laboratories in America developed the *transistor*. This is a compact device that can transmit a controlled electronic pulse through substances, like silicon, that are *semiconductors*. They act partly as a good conductor of electricity and partly as an insulator.

Transistors first impinged on the public consciousness in portable radios – the 'tranny'. Transistors could replace valves in other electronic devices, including computers. These transistorised computers formed the *second generation.*

At first, there was just one transistor per chip. Then more and more circuits were integrated onto a chip. *Integrated circuits (i/cs)* were the basis for *third generation* computers.

The number of transistors per chip rapidly grew from tens, to hundreds, to thousands, to tens of thousands, to hundreds of thousands. Each level of integration was known according to its *Scale of Integration (SI),* starting with Small, then moving through Medium, Large and Very Large (abbreviated to SSI, MSI, LSI and VLSI).

The more transistors that can be integrated into a smaller space, the more processing power and memory can be crammed onto a chip. It is these increasing levels of integration that has primarily accounted for the rapid hardware advances in information technology.

VLSI marks the start of the *fourth generation* of computer hardware. The fourth generation was also signified by the start of a rethink in computer construction – a movement away from the *von Neumann architecture* of EDVAC with its single CPU. Designs with multiple and parallel processors, together with new approaches to operating systems and database managment were also part of fourth generation developments.

The *fifth generation,* as defined in a Japanese government report of 1979 (see Chapter 6), moves further away from von Neumann machines.

The telecoms connection

Without telecommunications, the electronic office would consist of a lot of people and technology with nowhere to go. The technological roots of telecommunications stretch back to tom-toms and smoke signals but really get underway with the invention of the telegraph by the Englishmen Cooke and Whetstone in 1837. Almost forty years later, Scotsman Alexander Graham Bell contributed the telephone to the communications explosion.

Wireless transmissions were first made by Gugliemo Marconi in 1895 in his native Italy. Then another Scot, John Logie Baird, gave the first practical demonstration of television in 1926. The British Broadcasting Corporation transmitted the first public TV programmes in 1934. The first communications satellite was launched in America in 1963 – the idea of satellite communications having been conceived by science fiction writer Arthur C. Clark in 1945.

There are two main technologies in telecommunications – the *transmission* medium used to send information and the *switching* method used to connect devices in a network.

Radio waves, laser light beams and microwaves are examples of transmission media which do not have physical connections. Traditionally, telephones have been linked by copper cables, typically in pairs of twisted wires.

You could think of information flowing down a communications link like water in a pipe. The wider the pipe, the more information can flow. Twisted copper pairs are a *narrowband* method; they can have about 1.5 million *bits per second (bps)*. *Coaxial cables*, with a thickish central conducting core and *optical fibres* that carry pulses of light through hair-thin glass fibres, are *wideband* transmission links. (These are used in cable TV, for example, to provide multi-channel TV). A single optical fibre can transmit about 1 billion bps and hundreds of thousands of fibres can fit in a single cable.

In the past, telephone, radio, TV and other transmission has been done by sending *analogue* wave patterns. To turn them into digital form, a *demodulator* has to be used; and a *modulator* changes digital data back to analogue. An integrated *modem* (*mod*ulator/*dem*odulator) usually does this job. Increasingly, however, digital transmission is being used for all forms of communications because it is more reliable and efficient than analogue means.

A packet for the switchboard operator

A human switchboard operator, who manually plugged two ends of a cord into the appropriate sockets in a board, was the first form of telephone switching mechanism. In 1889, an American undertaker, Almon B. Strowger, thought his operator was passing on information to a rival, so he developed an automatic exchange, still known as the Strowger.

The Strowger has a lot of mechanical rods and cogs which turn and jerk into position to make the connection. Strowger gradually began to be replaced by electronic components and then by computer-controlled switching, as in PABXs. The method of joining up circuits linked to individual devices via an exchange is known as *circuit switching*.

In computer networks, another method was developed which sends information in little packets. At the front of each packet is the 'address' of where it is going. The wrapping of the packet includes other information to ensure that it arrives intact at its destination. *Packet switching* is widely used for store and forward systems, as discussed in Chapter 2.

Local area networks use a variety of techniques that do not involve going through an exchange. For example, in *Ethernet*, a local network developed by the Xerox Corporation, devices linked to it are regarded as 'stations' that 'broadcast' information through a cable from whence it can be detected by the 'station' to which it is addressed.

A *ring network* sends information around a continuous loop. For example, the Cambridge Ring, which was invented at Cambridge University in England, carries information in little 'buckets' around the loop. When a device detects information being sent to it, it 'tips out' the appropriate bucket into its own memory.

Any type of computer-based electronic office device can be linked into a local network – word processors, microcomputers, VDUs, large computers, and so on.

The last round-up

Many strands are woven into the richness that is the fabric of information technology.

Charles Babbage, for example, used a development from automatic loom technology to provide him with an input storage method – the punched card. Joseph Maria Jacquard in France developed his Jacquard card as a way to control the rods of a loom to which thread was connected. Where there was a hole in the card, the rod would move; otherwise it would stay still. Punched cards survived as a computer input medium until the 1980s.

A variety of technologies were also tried out for main memory on early computers, including tubes of mercury through which sonic signals were sent, Cathode Ray Tubes and valves. In the 1960s, *core stores* were used, consisting of loops of wire around a magnetic core that could be magnetised in one of two directions to represent a bit. Main memory is still sometimes referred to as 'core'.

More recently, electronic synthesisers in rock and pop music, digital recording techniques for records and videos, and countless other activities have caught the software-and-chips fever. They all help to stimulate and nourish the continuing growth of information technology.

9 A to Z of new office technology

The following is a brief description of the main terms you may encounter when dealing with the electronic office, including some important abbreviations. You should also look in the index for a reference to the part of the book in which you can find out more about these words and also for terms not covered in this glossary.

Acoustic coupler	A device that allows you to link electronic systems via the ordinary telephone handset
AI	Artificial Intelligence
Algorithm	A set of rules, a computer program procedure or a mathematical formula that can be followed to perform a task or produce an answer
Alphanumeric	A mix of alphabetic, numeric and, possibly, punctuation marks and other characters
Analog/analogue	Representing numbers not just by digits but by some continually varying method, such as hands on a watch or sound waves down a telephone line
ANSI	American National Standards Institute; many ANSI computing standards are accepted internationally
Append	To add new information at the end of an existing document or file
Application	The task performed by a user of computer-based systems. Applications software deals directly with such activities

Archival storage	Information kept for infrequent reference and as a back-up in case something happens to current files
Artificial Intelligence	Techniques that try to get computers to 'think' and behave in a similar manner to people
ASCII	American Standard Code for Information Interchange widely used to store and transmit digital information
Assembler	Software that turns low-level language programs into machine code; also term used for an assembly language
Assembly language	Low level programming language similar to machine code but easier to use
Audio-conference	A meeting held in different locations with participants linked through voice communications and, possibly, facsimile
Backing store	Media, such as magnetic disks and tape, used to store large amounts of information
Back-up	Computing resources that can be used when something goes wrong with the main system
Bandwidth	Measure of the amount of information that can flow through a telecommunications channel (see *broadband, narrowband, voiceband, wideband*)
BASIC	Beginner's All-purpose Symbolic Instruction Code; widely available high level programming language, particularly suited to people with no previous programming experience
Baud	Equivalent to *bits per second*
Benchmark	A standard test to gauge performance of a system
Bi-directional	A printer that increases speed by printing when moving in both directions across a page

Binary	Any system that can be in one of two states, such as o/1 or on/off
Bit	A single binary number; abbreviation for *bi*nary digi*t*
Bits per second	Measurement of the speed of digital information passing through a tele-communications channel
Bootstrap	Routine needed to start up a computer system
bps	bits per second
Broadband	High volume telecommunications channel bandwidth
Bubble memory	Compact way of storing large volumes of computer information on magnetic bubbles in a thin film of material, like garnet
Bug	Error in a computer system
Bureau	Organisation that sells time and services on its computer systems or word processors
Bus	Method of transporting information between components within a computer system and connecting a computer to input, output and communications devices
Byte	8 bits
CAD	Computer Aided (Assisted) Design; systems used in offices for design drawing
CAFS	Contents Addressable File Store that provides an efficient way of retrieving information by direct reference to the contents of a file rather than via indirect indexes
CAI	Computer Aided (Assisted) Instruction; see CAL
CAL	Computer Aided (Assisted) Learning; software which automatically takes a student through a programmed course

CAM	Computer Aided (Assisted) Manufacturing; systems used in manufacturing applications; can be linked to CAD for CAD/CAM
Cartridge	Container for magnetic disks and tape; also for programmed ROM with some computers
CAT	Computer Aided (Assisted) Training; see CAL
CCITT	Consultative Committee on International Telephones and Telegraph; an international body that sets many telecommunications standards
Chip	Tiny, smaller-than-thumbnail piece of material (usually silicon) on which transistors can be integrated into circuits to create computer processors and memory
chps	*ch*aracters *p*er *s*econd
Circuit switching	Means of connecting devices in a telecommunications network by linking the devices' transmission circuits via switching exchanges
COBOL	COmmon Business Oriented Language; a high level language widely used to write business applications programs
Columnar working	Word processing ability to manipulate information in columns
COM	Computer Output to Microfilm; archival store on microfilm
Compatibility	The ability of software and hardware to be moved to and linked to different systems and devices
Compiler	Software that translates high level language programs into machine code
Concurrency	Operating system's ability to handle many tasks at the same time

Core	An outdated synonym for 'main memory'; dates from when memory was made up of cells with magnetisable cores, called core store
Correspondence quality	Hard copy good enough to send as a letter outside an organisation
cps	*c*haracters *p*er *s*econd
CPU	Central Processing Unit, the main unit that performs calculations and controls the sequence of operations performed by the computer
Crash	A computer breakdown
CRT	Cathode Ray Tube used in a VDU screen, just as in TV sets
Cursor	Pointer on a VDU screen
CWP	Communicating Word Processors
Daisy wheel	Letter quality printer which has print characters around a petal-like wheel
Data	Computerish word for 'information'
Data administrator	Co-ordinator of computerised files and databases using housekeeping routines, dictionaries and other aids
Databank	Large database
Database	Large volumes of information stored on a computer system in a structured form
Data prep(aration)	Clerical task of creating computer input on punched cards, paper tape or magnetic media for subsequent input; data prep is being replaced by direct data entry
Data processing	Computerised tasks involving a great deal of structured routine work, such as payroll processing and accounting; associated with mainframe computing and DP Departments
Data steward	Union/staff representative on technical systems design team

DBMS	DataBase Management System; software and other techniques for creating and using databases
Debug	To look for and correct bugs (errors)
Decision Support System	Software modelling, information retrieval and other techniques that aid a decision-maker to reach a conclusion
Dictionary	Central element in database and word processing software to co-ordinate system; dictionaries in word processing could contain hyphenation rules, spelling aids or common translations
Digital	Representing quantities by discrete (separate) numbers or signals (analogue techniques use continuous signals)
Direct access	Ability to go straight to where information is held, say to a track on disk
Direct data entry	Inputting information directly to a computer without going through a data preparation phase
Directory	Word processing feature to help manage information on backing store, containing, for example, document names and lengths
Disk	Floppy or hard, magnetically coated disk used for computer input, output and storage
Disk drive	Unit used to read from and write to a disk
Disk pack	Container with a number of hard disks on a spindle
Diskette	A floppy disk
Display	Screen to display information, usually used in conjunction with a keyboard or other input device
Distributed processing	Computer system or network where processing power is at many locations, not centralised; also called distributed data processing

Document assembly/merge	Creating a document on a word processor by merging pre-stored standard text and freshly typed material
DOS	Disk(-based) Operating System provided and stored on disk
Dot matrix	Printer (usually near letter quality) which forms characters as a pattern of closely spaced dots
DP	Data Processing
DSS	Decision Support System
Dumb terminal	A terminal without its own computer memory or processor
Dump	Periodical copying of information to backing store as a standby if something goes wrong with the current information store
Duplex	Telecommunications link that allows transmission to take place in both directions at the same time
ECMA	European Computer Manufacturers Association; body which sets some internationally agreed standards
Editing	Ability to add, alter, move around and otherwise revise text with word processing; also used to change programs during software development
Editor	Software that allows you to carry out editing activities
EDP	Electronic Data Processing; equivalent to DP
EFTS	Electronic Funds Transfer System that allows financial transactions to be carried out in purely electronic form
Electronic filing	Carrying out filing and retrieval of documents and information using electronic devices and software

Electronic mail	Sending messages, documents and other information using electronic transmission, storage and output
Electronic mailbox	Facility to store electronic mail for subsequent forwarding to recipient
Electronic office	General term covering developments in computer-based systems used in office work
Electronic typewriter	Typewriter with limited storage, editing and display capabilities
Electrosensitive	Printing using specially coated paper that can be sensitised to produce an image; quiet but with relatively low quality print
Emulation	A system behaving like another; can be used to predict behaviour of a new service before it is installed
End user	The person who operates or otherwise uses a complete computing system or service
End-user language	Means of creating programs using commands and procedures natural to the users, who may be unaware they are generating programs
Enhanced matrix	Means of producing better-than-usual dot matrix printing by having dots overlapping
Ergonomics	Method of analysing how people and technology act at work to produce satisfying and safe, effective and efficient systems and work environments
Ethernet	Form of local area network
Executive terminal	Workstation designed specially for managerial tasks
Expert system	System programmed to 'think' with the logical reasoning of an experienced human expert in a specialised subject
Facsimile	A 'telecopier' transmission of the image of a document from one device to another via electronic telecommunications

Fax	Abbreviation for facsimile
Fibre optics	Means of electronic communications by sending pulses of light down hair-thin glass fibres bound together in a cable
Fiche	Microfilm in the form of a rectangular 'card'
File processing	Type of data management where information is held in separate files; less flexible and efficient than full database management systems
Firmware	Program stored in fixed 'hardwired' form in a ROM
Floppy disk	Flexible magnetic disk kept in permanent dust jacket
Flowchart	Graphical representation of the functions and sequence of actions to carry out a procedure, or to illustrate how a system or database is organised. Structured design uses different forms of chart. The flowchart below is a simplified summary of basic word processing routines. You start at the top and follow the arrows. At the diamond-shape box a choice of route is made, depending on the answer to the question. (see chart opposite)
Font (or Fount)	Particular design of printer or typewriter characters
Form design	Word processing ability to design and store document formats leaving specific areas open for text to be input subsequently
Full page display	VDU screen that can show a full A4 page of text; other screens are typically about half this length.
G	Giga – 1 billion (1 000 million)
Gateway	Link between two independent information networks

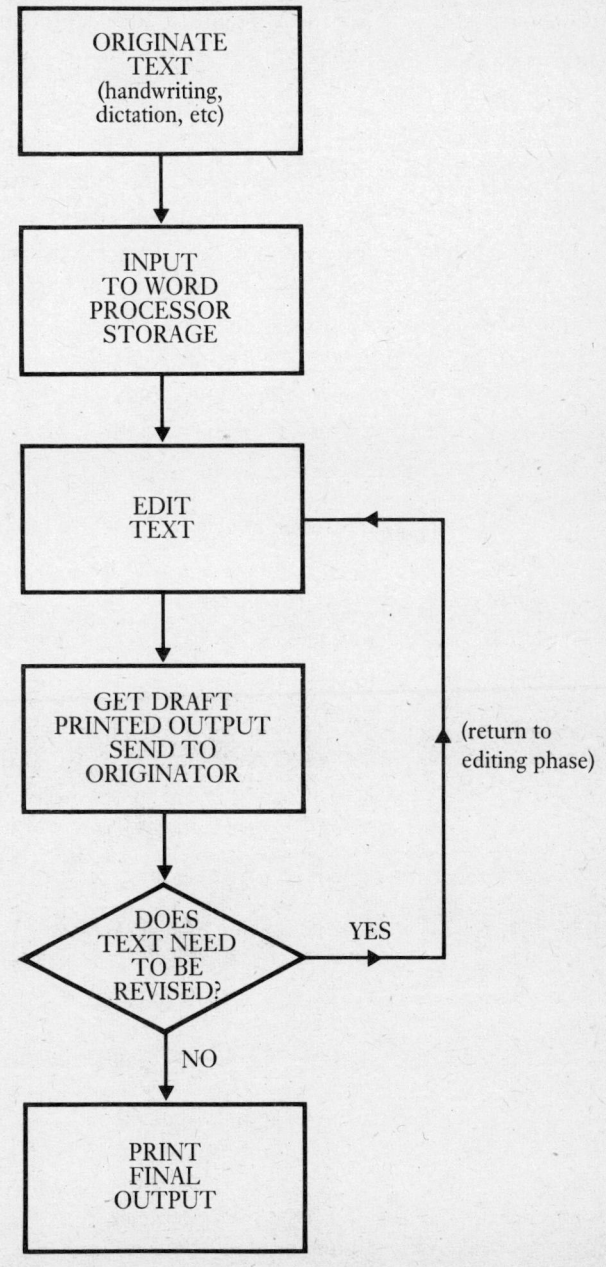

Ghost cursor — Secondary pointer available on some word processors that appears when doing a secondary task during input or editing; main cursor fades when ghost is on the screen

GIGO — Garbage In, Garbage Out; warning that wrong information will produce incorrect results however good the computer

Global exchange — Automatically changing a word or phrase wherever it appears in the text.

Graceful degradation — Ability of system to keep running even if some parts fail

Graphics — Pictures, drawings, graphs and other information that is not pure text and numbers

Half duplex — Telecommunications link that allows transmission in both directions but not at the same time

Hard copy — Printed output from a computer system

Hard disk — Rigid magnetic disk for storing information

Hardware — Physical equipment

Hardwired — Fixed electronic circuit patterns to carry out a programmed task

Hertz — Measurement of number of cycles per second when a signal is frequently repeated, for example, in the refresh rate of a VDU display

High level language — Programming language using words (usually in English) and procedures similar to those used in the application being pro-grammed

Housekeeping routines — Software that helps organise available resources; in word processing allows docu-ments to be removed, deleted, re-arranged on backing store

Human factors engineering — Study of how people and technology can work in harmony; basically the same as ergonomics

Hyphenation	Word processing facility that automatically decides where words are to be hyphenated at the end of a line
Hz	Hertz
Icon/ikon	Symbol on a screen representing a particular function
IEEE	Institute of Electrical and Electronics Engineers; US body responsible for many internationally agreed standards
Impact printer	Printer that creates image by hitting print head onto paper – a daisy wheel printer, for example
Information centre	Place within an organisation that provides advice on, and access to, computerised services
Information provider	Organisation, group or individual who provides information to a viewdata system
Information retrieval	Automatic search for information stored in computerised form and presentation of extracted information on an appropriate output device
Ink jet printer	Printer that creates characters by droplets of ink squirted at high speed onto paper
Input	Getting information into a computer-based system
Intelligent copier/printer	Device which combines word processing, OCR and fax capabilities
Intelligent terminal	Terminal with its own memory and processor
Interactive	System that immediately responds to input in a continuous user/system dialogue
Interactive video	Form of CAL that uses video tape or disk controlled by software
Interface	Boundary between two entities, such as between software or hardware modules or between the user and the system

Interpreter	Type of compiler that translates high level language programs statement-by-statement, rather than requiring the whole program before it can start
Interrupt	When CPU stops to handle I/O or communications task
I/O	Input/Output
ISO	International Standards Organisation; responsible for many computer standards
Justification	Word processing facility to make sure that text lines up evenly at right hand (or left hand) margin
K	Kilo – 1000; or 1 024 (2^{10}) where binary calculations are involved, as occurs when measuring computing capacity
Keyboard	Set of keys used for input
Keypad	Input device with a few keys – ten digits and a few control keys for example
Key-to-disk/ tape	Data preparation that creates disk or tape information by input from a keyboard
Keyword search	Searching through computerised information by specifying the words that identify what items are being looked for
Kips	Thousands (K) of *i*nstructions *p*er *s*econd, a measurement of computer speed
Laser printer	Very high speed printer that creates characters with lasers on light-sensitive material
LCD	Liquid Crystal Display; a display made by activating a liquid crystal substance; used in flat screens, such as in portable computers and calculators
LED	Light Emitting Diode; a semiconductor display suitable for flat screens but requiring more power that LCDs

Letter quality	Hard copy good enough to send as a letter outside an organisation
Light pen	Used to 'draw' graphics input
Line printer	Printer that produces output a line at a time
Local	Computing capability close to the end user
Local (area) network	Interlinking devices within a building or single site
Logging on/off	Procedures for starting up an interactive dialogue and for terminating the session; usually includes giving a secret password when logging on
Low level language	Programming language similar in structure to machine code but easier to use; also called assembler or assembly language
LSI	Large Scale Integration; chips containing quite a high number of bits or processor circuits but not as many as VLSI
M	Mega – 1 million or 1 048 576 (2^{20}) where binary calculations are involved, as occurs when measuring computing capacity
Machine code	Numeric codes of a computer's basic instructions
Magnetic card/disk/tape	Devices with magnetic coating that store digital information according to the direction of tiny magnets in the surface; collectively known as magnetic media
Main memory	Memory for information needed immediately by the processor
Mainframe	Computer larger than a minicomputer or small business system
Margination	Word processing capability to set margins automatically by specifying where lines begin and end
Mass storage	Backing store with very large amounts of information

Matrix output	Formation of characters on a printer or screen as a pattern of tiny dots
Memory	Sometimes used synonymously with 'storage' but usually applies to main memory rather than backing store
Menu	Method of user/system interaction that presents a menu of numbered items from which the user selects
MICR	Magnetic Ink Character Recognition; an input method using characters printed in special ink and typefaces, as used on the bottom of cheques
Micro	Abbreviation for microchip, microprocessor and microcomputer
Microcomputer	Smallest and cheapest complete computer with processor, main memory, input, output and (possibly) communications capability
Microfiche	Same as fiche
Microfilm	Used to store reduced images of documents
Microprocessor	A computer processor on a chip
Mini(computer)	A computer roughly between a microcomputer and mainframe in capability and price; often incorporated into other systems and products
Mips	*M*illions of *i*nstructions *p*er *s*econd, a measurement of computer speed
MIS	Management Information System; software to cope with a variety of management, administrative and accounting tasks
Modelling	Techniques that work out the likely behaviour of a system and consequences of taking various decisions

Modem	*Mo*dulator/*dem*odulator; a device needed to translate between analogue and digital signals when communicating between computer-based devices over analogue transmission links
Module	A self-contained unit, part of a larger system
MOS	Metal Oxide Semiconductor; a chip with layers of a metal, an oxide and a semi-conductor to make transistors
Mouse	Device that moves the cursor on a screen in the direction in which the mouse is rolled along a surface
MTBF	Mean Time Between Failures; the average length of time between breakdowns of the system
Multifunction workstation	Workstation from which a variety of different types of task can be carried out
Multi-programming	Operating system's ability to handle more than one program at a time
Multi-window	Ability of a screen to display more than one document or task
Nano	One billionth (1 000 millionth)
Narrowband	Low capacity telecommunications channel
Natural language	Language used by people; such as English, Hindi or French
Network	The interlinking through switching centres of a variety of devices and computer systems
NLQ	Near Letter Quality; printer output not as good as letter quality but still acceptable for most purposes
Node	Switching centre in a network or any point in a diagram where a number of lines meet

Non-impact printer	Printer that creates characters without a print-head hitting the paper, such as electrosensitive, ink jet and thermal
NTA	New Technology Agreement; a framework for management/union negotiations about technological change
Number cruncher	A very large computer that mainly deals with complex numerical calculations, such as those involved in weather forecasts
OCR	Optical Character Recognition; an input method that automatically reads printed characters, sometimes expecting them to be in a special OCR typeface
OEM	Original/Other Equipment Manufacturer; a company that supplies systems that include key components, or a complete computer, from another supplier
Office automation	Sometimes used synonymously with 'the electronic office' but implies an orientation towards production-line automation
Offline	Computing activities carried out when not directly linked to another system
OMR	Optical Mark Reading; an input method that identifies marks at particular positions on a document
Online	Linked directly to another system
OOF	Office Of the Future; a synonym for 'the electronic office'
Open systems	Information networks built to standards which allow different types and makes of systems to be linked together
Operating system	Software that organises the resources of the system and co-ordinates work run on it
Optical fibre	Hair-thin glass fibres used in fibre optic communications

OSI	Open Systems Interconnection; an ISO standard structure to give users more freedom in interconnecting devices
Output	Getting information out of a computer-based system
PABX	Private Automatic Branch eXchange; automatic (now usually computer-controlled) exchange used within an organisation for telephones and other communications
Packet switching	Transmission of information encoded as 'packets' with the address of the destination at the front, which is used to route the packet through switching exchanges
Paper tape	Punched paper tape was an early form of storage, input and output
Parameter	A factor in a program that can vary according to the value given to it; parameter-driven software allows users to tailor system by giving values to various parameters
Password	Codeword or number checked by some systems before allowing someone to use their facilities
PBX	Private Branch eXchange; sometimes synonymous with PABX but usually a non-computerised exchange
PCM	Plug Compatible Manufacturer; a supplier who makes peripherals, storage and processors that behave in the same way as those from a major manufacturer
Peripherals	Input, output and storage devices
Personal computer	Microcomputer or workstation used primarily for an individual's own applications rather than corporate tasks
Personal computing	Capability for doing personal-computer-type activities from a terminal linked to shared computing capabilities

Petal printer	A daisy wheel printer
Phototypesetter	A computer-based device that produces material ready to be photographed for high quality printing
PIN	Personal Identification Number; a password used with plastic cards, as in an automatic cash dispenser
Plotter	Output device for drawing graphs
Port	Point at which input, output, storage and communications connections can be made to a computer
Portability	Ability to move software between different machines
PoS terminal	Point of Sale terminal located at the place where a sale is made, such as at a super-market checkout
Positive presentation	Screen that has black characters on a white background
Printer	Output device to produce printed hard copy
Printout	Output from a computer-controlled printer
Processor	Hardware unit that performs calculations and controls actions of the system according to software instructions
Program	Detailed instructions that automatically control the operation of a computer; collectively known as software
Programmed correspondence	Word processing ability to store text for subsequent inclusion in a document
Programming language	Language with precisely defined commands, statements and syntax used for writing programs
Proportional spacing	Ability to have letters of different widths, with 'm' the widest and 'i' the narrowest

Protocol	Clearly defined set of rules and procedures gone through when communicating between computerised devices
PSTN	Public Switched Telephone Network; the standard telephone service for home and business subscribers
PTT	Post, Telephone and Telegraph; the major, often government owned, national tele-communications authority
Punched card/tape	Input, output and storage media with information represented as holes in a card or paper tape
QBE	Query-By-Example; a way of retrieving information by specifying items being looked for in appropriate positions of a standard format displayed on a VDU screen
Query languages	Commands and procedures used to retrieve information from a database
QWERTY	First five letters in top alphabetic row on a keyboard; AZERTY and QWERTZ are variations used in other countries
RAM	Random Access Memory; main memory on a chip which can be written to, updated and read from by user programs
Random access	Going straight to the place where information is held
Real time system	A system capable of responding instan-taneously to a request or event
Relational database	One type of database management system that has great flexibility in establishing relations between different elements in the database
Remote	Computing capability away from a central computer but close to the user

Repeat key	Word processing function that allows a character to be repeated many times without continually re-keying it
Report generator	Software that makes it easy to change the format of displayed or printed output
Response time	Time between a user's input and the response in an interactive system
Restore	To re-create files from the state in which they were last dumped before an error or breakdown occured
Reverse video	Highlighting parts of a screen by reversing the normal foreground/background colours
Rigid disks	Hard magnetic disks
Ring	Form of local area network
ROM	Read Only Memory; main memory on a chip which can only be read from by a user program, not written to or updated
RS-232	Input/output port standard common to many microcomputers
Run	What a program does when it is performing
S-100	Standard bus of 100 lines used by many microcomputers
Scrolling	Moving the 'window' shown on a screen up or down (vertically), left or right (horizontally) to see text in other parts of a document
Search and replace	'Global exchange', automatically replacing a word or phrase wherever it appears in a document with new text
Semiconductor	Substance used for transistors that acts partly as a conductor and partly as an insulator of electronic pulses; silicon is the most widely used in microelectronics
Serial access	Searching through all stored information from its beginning to get to the point you want, as with magnetic tapes

Shared logic/ resources	Sharing processing, storage and output between more than one word processor or workstation
Silicon	Constituent of sand, most popular semi-conductor for chips
Simplex	Communications link that allows trans-mission to take place only in one direction at a time
Simulation	Mimicking the behaviour of one system on another, say using software and mathe-matical modelling techniques
Single-line display	Display used with electronic typewriters to show current line being input
Socio-technical design	Method and approach to systems design which gives as much priority to human, organisational and long-term aspects as to technical and short-term economic require-ments
Software	Programs that (automatically) control how a computer operates
Solid state	Electronic device with no mechanical moving parts
Sort	Software that can automatically put infor-mation into an ordered sequence, such as an alphabetical one
Specification	Detailed definition, often including flow-charts and other diagrams, of a system's objectives, structure and working procedures
Split screen	Ability to display more than one 'window' on a screen at time to show different docu-ments or functions
Spooling	Another word for 'offline'
Spreadsheet software	Software, usually used for financial model-ling, that allows input to be made by keying values into a 'cell' in a grid of rows and columns

Stand-alone	Self-sufficient system with its own processor, storage and output
Standard text	Frequently used text that can be stored for subsequent use in assembling documents with a word processor
Stand-by	A duplicate system or part of a system that can swing into action if the live system breaks down
Storage	A device for storing information to be input to a computer
Store and forward	Telecommunications method that first stores information before sending it to the recipient when required
String	A group of alphanumeric characters
Strip window	A display that shows a single line of text
Structured design	A systematic and well-documented method of designing a flexible, easy-to-maintain system based on self-contained modules
Structured programming	Developing software to a structured design
Systems analysis	Process of analysing how a systems works and how a new system should operate
Systems design	Analysing and specifying the organisational structures, work routines, job functions and technical requirements of a system
Systems house	Company which sells a total system, often including hardware from other suppliers
Systems software	Programs concerned with organising and running a system's resources, rather than carrying out applications tasks
Tab rack	Line at the top of a word processing screen to define tab and margin settings, equivalent to metal tabs at the back of a manual typewriter
Tablet	Flat board used as part of input devices, particularly for graphics input

Tape, magnetic or paper	Used for input, output and storage
Taylorism	Scientific managment techniques used in manufacturing production line automation; characterised by jobs that repeat a limited range of simple tasks
Technology agreement	Conceived by trade unions as a framework for negotiating conditions under which technological change takes place
Technology representative	Union/staff representative on technical systems design team
Tele-communications	Information transmission using electronics, sound and other means that do not involve physical transportation
Tele-conferencing	Meetings by telecommunications between many parties in different locations
Teletex	International standard that enables word processors to link with the traditional telex network
Teletext	Videotex broadcast from a central point to receiving sets, such as TV sets with special adaptors
Telex	Long established form of relatively slow electronic mail with keyboard input and printer output
Terminal	Device linked to a computer or other devices in an information network
Text processing	Computer-based handling of textual information; a more apt term for 'word processing'
Thermal printing	Printing mechanism that uses heated elements on heat-sensitive paper to create character images
Transistor	Device that acts like a switch or amplifier in an electronic circuit; abbreviation for *trans*fer re*sistor*

Typebasket	Nest of type hammers which is the print mechanism in manual typewriters
Typeface	A particular design of characters used in a printer or typewriter
User friendly	System which is easy to use and understand by a newcomer to computing
Utility software	Programs that do general system housekeeping
VAN	Value Added Network; which provides information services to subscribers, such us electronic mail, in addition to basic transmission and switching of data
Variable	Element in a program or equation that can be given different values
VDT	Visual Display Terminal; another term for VDU
VDU	Visual Display Unit; a device with keyboard and screen
Video-conferencing	A teleconference that links participants in separate locations by picture, voice and, possibly, facsimile
Video disk/tape	Devices, similar to those used for video home entertainment, which can store and give access to still or moving images for electronic filing and CAL
Video terminal	Another term for VDT or VDU
Videotex	General term for information services that store, send and display text and graphics; viewdata is interactive videotex, teletext is broadcast videotex
Viewdata	Videotex that allows the user to interact by sending messages to the system
Virtual	A facility or resource that does not physically exist but which is simulated so that the user can act as if it does exist

Virtual memory/storage	Operating system's ability to enable programs to run although there is not as much real memory available as it expects
Voicegram/memo	Electronic mail facility to store and send speech mixed with text messages
Voice recognition	Input by direct human speech
Voice response	Computer-controlled speech output
VS	Virtual Storage
WAN	Wide Area Network that covers many geographical areas and buildings
Wideband	High capacity telecommunications channel
Winchester disk	A compact hard disk held in a sealed cartridge
Word	A unit of computer memory. It can be 8 bits, 16 bits or 32 bits in length as far as most personal or small business computers are concerned
Word processing	Computer-based system that stores, edits, outputs and transmits typed information
Word processor	Device purpose-built for, and often dedicated to, word processing tasks; consists of a keyboard and screen plus editing software
Workstation	Device (or a desk with a number of devices) from which electronic office work takes place
WP	Word Processing/Processor
Wraparound	Word processing ability that automatically starts a new line, during typing, when text reaches the right hand margin
X25	CCITT standard for packet switching transmission
Zero suppression	Ability to stop the printing of zeros before the first digit in a number, for example, '164.96' not '0000164.96'

Index